ARTSCOPE

Stargazey Pie © *Peter Flux 2011*

The moral right of the author has been asserted

Also by this author:
Experimental Work: (with collaboration with others):
The Twilight Timepiece Sunburst Kid
And Short Stories:
Back-garden Sniping Across The Universe
Sci-Fi Short Story Compilations by <u>Pete</u> Flux:
A Fossil In The Rock
Alien Skies
Also available in Ltd Editions Books:
Other Work (Novel):
The Secret Poems of the Montevidean
by the Count of Lautréamont the Second (*Le Phenix*)

ISBN 978-0-9554479-1-4
British Library Cataloguing Publication Data: a CIP catalogue record for
this book is available from the British Library (also Website).

First Edition
Published by Artscope Publications

Main Text Font set in 10pt Ariel Rounded MT Bold

Ltd Editions Books
Torbay, Devon, UK

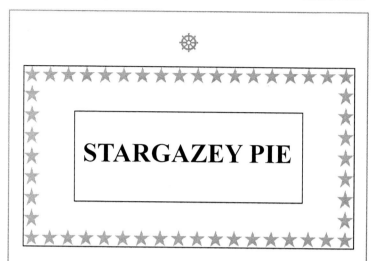

STARGAZEY PIE

*A Selected Compilation
of Poems
by*

Peter Flux

ARTSCOPE

ARTSCOPE PUBLICATIONS

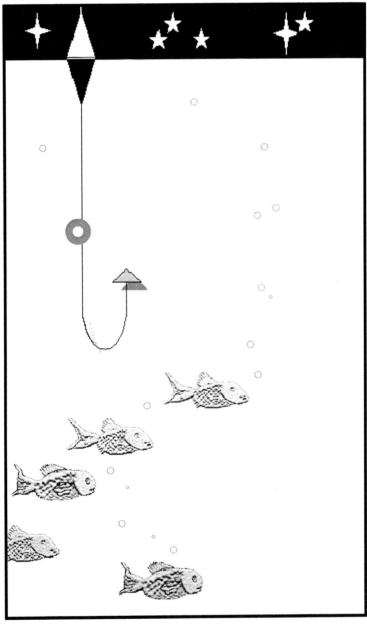

Peter Flux

STARGAZEY PIE

Selected Poems

Dedications

To my daughters; *Ginger* is for Rachel Flux, who ranks up there with the *very best* artists of which I have ever known, read about or seen exhibited; and *Thar She Blows!* is for my darling Jana, a truly wonderful woman. *There She Dances* is for *both* of these 'gals'!

Pixikin-led By Starshine I wish to dedicate to my granddaughter Grace Leila Mary Hanley, with *much* love, (from Gramps!).

The River Sacred And A Tree is dedicated to the memory of *Pyp*, elegant and courageous Sioux of courageous spirit, who passed to Happy Hunting in 1992 aged only 43: (Hey woman! *Revolution* IS *Poetry!*). *The Waves Don't Part* is dedicated to memory of my father, *Bruce Henry Flux*, who passed in 1991; (a penny for the Old Guy!).

Other dedications are as follows: *Stargazey Pie* is for Jane and Jonnie Bull, star-footed companion-travellers of the mystic agéd path; *Forever Cove: (Your Dream Is Over)* is dedicated to artist, writer and musician John Ono Lennon, and *In Memory of Them* to Yoko Ono Lennon; *Vampire* is dedicated to Barbara Steele; *For Certain Sure* is a dedication to Mary Webb, the quilled sprite; *The Frail Abandoned Muse Of Grace* is to Jean Cocteau, artist, 'head' and writer-poet; *Ghost On The Rocks* is to the memory of the *beatific* Jack Kerouac; *The Vortex Bird* is to the late Joseph Chief Fools Crow (Hey! Are those my much-loved mirror-shades of old?); *The Awakening Of Water* is dedicated to Lord Byron, poppy-footed poet; and *Written* is to Percy Bysshe Shelley, the lightning-hearted fellow-traveller; and last, but not least, *Under The Moon* is to Christine Heaney who provided unique service in writing its text down from sleepy dictation upon my waking!

To all, thank you deeply, *always...!*   *P.F.*

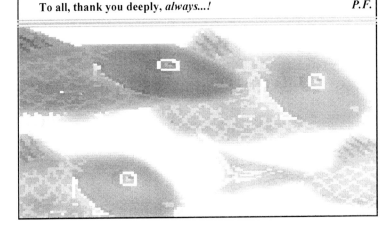

2

CONTENTS

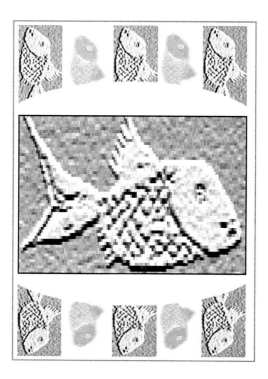

(200 Poem Titles)

CONTENTS

Introduction

Amazed that I *could*, I began writing poems in Nineteen Eighty Seven, while living in Islington, North London.

The poems in *Stargazey Pie* are of various nature, and are written under varying 'styles', moods of inspiration, and circumstance of writing. For example, *Choux Dream Poem* was written down upon waking from sleep. I dreamt the whole piece, exactly as rendered, and only had to write it down immediately as consciousness returned. In my dream, each letter was made of choux pastry, and set out in the lines of the piece upon a large, black baking tray! (I have meant to actually carry this out in choux pastry, and make a version in some material more resilient to the ravages of time, but this remains, to date, yet to carry out). Also from that place of dreams, the first lines of *Under The Moon* were dictated upon waking, being written down verbatim; (for further see 'Dedications', p. 2).

Dawn Horus Poem was originally called *Dawn Horus*, but as this became a title of my extant Science Fiction short story, the word 'Poem' was added to the verse. Of the poems which should receive further mention or explanation, the work titled *Forever Cove: (Your Dream Is Over)* was conceived as being set to sound (not necessarily music, as such). The work titled *Street of Dreams* was written after it became known that Lennon died when he was at the beginning of writing a song named *Street of Dreams*. Although I've never read Lennon's *Street of Dreams*, or even know if this is currently extant, my poem given here is an attempt at 'filling the gap left'. Using the same title, it attempts to provide fitting imagery. The poem could also be performed as a song.

I hope that *you* find much pleasure and continued diversion in your reading of these wonky works!

Peter Flux.

Selected Poems

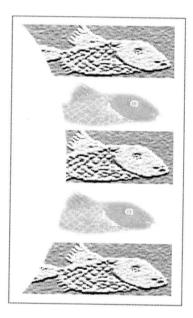

First: *(Punk Poem)*

This is the first day of Spring
A lilt in tune of promised Summers.
The sky stands tall to display all
Look! first word first page first book!

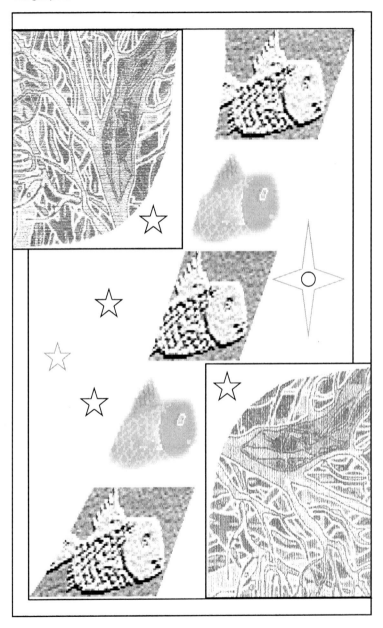

Stargazey Pie

Down through the roots of trees,
Down through earth, loam,
Mould and stone,
Past bones to molten lees, and on,
Roars the furnace core
Which once formed inner stuff of stars
As did you or I... *Yes!...*
Even creatures of Jupiter or Mars....
Hidden suns the planets hold,
Lava, rocks and fine-spun gold,
Diamonds hard among cracked bones,
And if you listen well, listen clear,
For the sound of aeons' very marrow,
You may cipher, faintly hear,
Down All Tomorrows
And down through the roots of years
The sap of all sad sorrows.

Down through roots of living blood,
Down through space and rocks,
Flesh and mud,
Past bones to melted heart,
Churns the blind core
Of hidden light and heat and more
That shows the mask of Earth
To rushing air, its swirling cloud
Fingerprints of unseen hands,
As the round face of changing sky
Becomes a loud *Shout!...* a cry
That lands a lasting memory
Diamond strong to baste stars' song
About the far-flung firmament;
And if you listen deep, listen strong,
You may cipher, faintly scent,
Down All Tomorrows,
Down through years' life-long weep,
The melt of all sad sorrows, spent.

11

Down through the roots of plants,
Down through each comet's thrust
Fire and dust,
Past glazed fish-eyes entranced,
This blind clock's face
Of Time-baked crust
That transforms the dreams of stars
Pure star-grain waters race and dance
Close to sand of beaches found
Diamond quiet; put face to ground,
And if you listen good,
As mute as dusk,
As still as wood,
(Shush! now... without a sound!)
You may cipher, faintly ask
And understand...
Down All Tomorrows,
Down through hung tears of icicles,
The hum of all sad sorrows, and,
Down through Time-grain rings of trees
The voice of Earthly legacies,
In amber star-born chronicles....

Opening The Door

Opening the door
The stars suspend
Walking into the essence
Stillness across the beach
The silence filled with sounds
All Existence by blessing
In breath, in awe of night
Beneath tall echoes
Seabirds dim in the dark
Winging the Universe
Marvellous the mundane
This One Time always
The world never sleeps
The stars suspend.

We That Have No Home

We that have no home
In all the living Universe,
Never can we bravely roam
Until the centre we find within us
Crystal clear.

Be it here, or some place afar
Where we, wondering, wander go,
Walking Earth or around
Some faint star distant,
I can tell you this, for this I Know,
And know this very instant...
Never do we constant roam,
Until the radiant heart we find within us
Crystal clear,
For only then have we found our home,
Here,
In all the gleaming Universe.

The Dreamful Stars

Climb a glazed and spiral stairway
To walk the dreamful stars,
To window soft as starlight through
Clouds in highest, lightest thought,
Float upon the golden air holding
Silvered the top of the world.

So when you come to open
Sleep-soaked eyes, awake in wonder
Upon your broken-ladder bed,
You shall fond remember a freedom,
Lived and settled in experience,
Nestled within newly-feathered arms.

Night Owls

White owls meet in night-air skies,
Beat feather-wing feather snowflake sound
As the Sleepers, tight close to ground,
Dream weightless rise,
Lift
And soar
While in astral ears oceans roar,
Rift, drift
To gather flying around with opened ears,
Gift cloud nests of all their dream-time years.

Owls eddy across the city,
Alight
With stilled black-air glide,
Swoop and slide
Over buildings to trees
In parks and streets where they hide,
Blow and breeze
Their clawed flightless fur-dread wide
Fears, damask leaf dismays, fright,
Sing screaming, adrift....

Of these other flyers in their night,
Heard first with bird-sharp ears:
Then owls hawk-eye
Squawk as they spy
The etheric Sleepers walk, glowing bright,
Growing moonbeams from every pore,
Neon rays in splays
Searching torch-gleam dream,
As they plumb and explore
Their soft slumbering
Universal crèche
In lumbering,
In weaving mesh,
In wheeling wheeled
Round circle ways.

Then as one, with owlish dare,

Two, five, eight,
Ten and more birds mount
Upward
Through vibrate playful air,
Go fount,
Go twist and turn to moon about
In wide-eyed wit to woo
Buoyant beaming twinkled,
Ripped, fanned and wrinkled,
Rip Van Winkled,
Bobbing bodies of the Sleepers who
Plane and awn,
Sport and play,
Reeling with happy owls in float
Flight, until the yawn throat
Feeling day
Beaks sun dawn
Crack through the last black
Remnant rags of fleeing
Night, as lack-light fades away....

And, as tired owls at last
Close well-primed ghost nocturnal eyes,
The Sleepers, drowned dreams passed,
Forgetful rise
Into fast
And often
Howling days of flight forgotten.

Lava Me Down

Lava me down to sea lap,
Lava me down to crack of rock-salt
Under blistered sun,
Lava me down to spray solid, growl of ocean
Cowled upon rounded planet head,
Here, where seabirds sail and soar,
Sing screaming, adrift....

Sea Timescape

Behind Time's fixed and bony grin,
Deep under the taut skin
Of the hiding, bristled sea,
Ancient air of past tears
Bubbles free, races
Upwards from the pea-green
Wreck of all the years,
Through the faces of ages greying,
Away from solemn seaweed...
Fishes playing.

Behind Time's fixed and hollow stare,
Deep within the hair
On the head of fluid Earth,
The riding, rising, unsaddled air
Bubbles free, bursts
Upward... breaks into chill first
Light's glow of all the days that dawned
Before night's black spraying,
Away from solemn seaweed...
Fishes playing.

Behind Time's fixed and linear mask,
Deep below eternal task
And tumble of the rapt sea dew,
Dolphins sing to ask
The dumb sky of the sound
Of land; and, between
The soft mew of stars,
(Heard by no earthly ear) jars
The jagged pound
Of a thousand bright meteors flaying
Toward solemn seaweed...
And fishes playing.

16

The Autumn Plough

The Autumn plough stands upon its tail,
Spoons up through the yawning sky,
Balanced fine and proud and pale
Poised on blackest horizon silent
That weaves a wire awry
In dance of trees beneath constellations old,
Ancient,
Stars metal-hard and rolled
Slow across to torch their fires,
Piercing light-years' layers
To reach by sure-faint touch the transient sight,
To pool within phials of eyes now bathed
In intoned essence,
In sounds of deepest prayers
As overhead sky's dial turns and tunes
Melodious in stellar matrimony,
A burn of suns in falling leafy light
Numberless in float of first and final flight
Throughout this clear chime of a night.

And behind the cloud mask
That blue day paves
Revolve these uncounted stars
Above spin of Earth, unseen,
In join of perfect harmony.

Tread Careful Now....

Hush! tread careful now the night is old
There are forces as would sheer to ash
In flake of hiding recesses where fitful fires
Light but dim the cave of 'morrow's caverns
In echoed silences of our sleeping darks!

Portrait Of A Winter's Moon

The moon bathes in the sea tonight,
Swirling waters her death shores clean,
Ancient dusts damp of ocean's might
Float free and down as in a dream
Of slow dance sand and snow;
And for all
Who have eyes to see,
See now
With glance and gleam:
Her reflected light does spin and fall
Its Autumn leaves from Winter's naked tree,
Serene.

Full moon breathes this black space night,
Billow cloud-breath takes form's cold shape,
Pillows pocked head in her second-hand light,
Shines waxy pale with stars at nape
Of unseen neck, void shoulders veiled in white;
And for all
Who have ears to hear,
Hear now with glance and gleam:
A frozen distress,
Her deflected scream does silent call
Through all deep emptiness,
Sharp and brittle-clear,
As some waning widow's last drying, dying tear.

Moon's bland beam opens dark soft night,
Makes of my hand a flattened thing,
Faint tremble wing,
Takes moot time to alight and silent sing,
Breaks half-tone glow over sleeping land,
An air caress unfelt by skin,
Until it first
Has made good melt
Of hidden thirst
Of heart:
And for all within

Who have nerves to feel,
Feel now its glance and gleam:
Undress the real sky's
Moon-mist shroud caul,
Bare and birth her free, unless
Her opal sheen is but a milk
Dream's fall,
A mirage silk
Spun of Emptiness....

Sleeper

The Sleepers cocooned
Around their glowing fires,
Chrysalides under their eyelids
Bathed in firelight,
Slumber under the stars
In the time-locked, lumbering night.

The Sleepers marooned
Sleep in glowing desires,
Pupas within their stupors
Bathed in starlight,
Slumber to space
Through the time-locked, lumbering night.

The Sleepers festooned
In dream's glowing face,
Wrapped with space-dust
Bathed in moons,
Trussed, beached around star-fires
In the time-locked, lumbering night,
Sleep on....

The Sleepers, dreaming thoughts now passed,
Again forgetful rise
And stumble into fast
And all-to-often
Too-bright days by sleep begotten.

Blood Earth

Blood earth,
The baked flesh of fields
Under the lemon-scented sun
Set in mackerel skies and soundless
Waves upon cerulean shores
Blanched in rounded bones...
A pebble moon arise.

Earth I could eat you
When at bask as this,
Swallow your mountains whole,
Drink your oceans,
Slurp your seas,
Quaff your rivers
As you breathe the flight of lovers
Under the black roof
Sailing through Nowhere as your course.

Earth you will eat me
As I task as this,
Take me down whole,
Drink me total,
Slurp my blood,
Quaff my spirit
As I breathe the love of flight
Under your black roof
Sailing through Nowhere as my course.

Blood earth,
The baked flesh of fields
Blanched in rounded bones
A pebble moon arise.

Crazy Gold

Crazy gold
Sunlight after a hard cold Winter
Where the chrysalis dreams hazy
Now sings the wing.
A late Spring breaking slumber.

Crazy gold
The breath the thoughts of trees
Where sap thrums tunes of future resin
Now brings an open flavour.
The taste the curl of leaves.

Crazy gold
Vanishing below awakened worlds
Where the mimic of sleep slow dims
Now rings this cloak around.
The dark rim brims in stars.

Crazy gold
Untouched nugget you touched me
Where you live in my skin
Now wearing your heat.
Hidden wealth of the cool soul night.

Shower

Rain spots upon dry stone,
Brings up colours of forgotten leaves,
Fallen Autumn flags ripened in ages,
Muted in moments,
Forgotten pages
Flutter once more,
Brief forests under quick Winter skies...
A shower of leaves.

Should I Return

Should I return and swim again
The toe-dipped seas of All Existence,
The strut and ebb of tip-toe upon this salted Earth
In tireless tread and footfall of the sunning grain;
Would I issue out again to wheel and reign,
Then sputtered flames might sprite about their olden,
                                        golden hearth
To warm me smiling inward as in a lover's glance.

Should I, stepping apprehensive, enhance the chance
To climb once more the Ever-spiral Stair
And newly bathe in dream-fall, lid-fall wash of Sleep,
Then Myths would comb with starfish their Years-long
                                        gilded hair
As lithe magnetic sirens wail from their sea-rock steep
To plait horizons slim-cut, so seaweed tissue thin,
And by these net strands rope me sweet,
Returned in Life to pulse and certain beat,
Spun and quick beneath the skin!

Nightheart

Where the oaken shadows umber
Elephantine beams lumber silent,
Motionless between moonlight
Sent through trees
Still pauses solidified, there
Stands breath-held heart of night....

The Arm That Holds The Slightest Breath

So shall you give the ungiven word
That soars above some spoken vowels
To describe the wings of thought
In ways yet poised in gathered spring
Now expanded to meet the fingertips
Of both horizons, the wind
Which crests the plumes of air
That rise and billow in the hair,
The tops of trees, the waves
In rage upon your shores, the breast
In heave and full of throat that speaks
Unuttered words, emotion spared the tongue
In flame or ice of passion full run
Sped to the zenith of all desire
Of being part of your marble flesh
Your immortal soul the soft peach gland
Everlasting
Through all event
The ditch
The hill
The humble plain
The torch of our entwining life
Root of enchanted breath
The ages birth a gasp of awe in the mouth
Through lips enshrined in wonder.

A roundness to play and ply the heavens
Has such a sound as whirring would not be mete
Nor humming touch the voice of suns
A-spin within the trim of space
Nor songs of suns the mottled spheres dare spin
Would show the face of circles thrown aloft
To the mortal eyes of galaxies and men
In thrall of time and time again
The mythology of stars adrift
In tales of the eternal moment.

Disc at movement upon the deep my heart
Between the light and dark the nature of this act
Shall wave a flag to banner above the thought
The soul of man's and woman's level
The unmetred metre the length uncut
In natural hug of the linear line untravelled
Or navigated by the final plot in sands
A-flow the gossamer of the breast unclothed
The shellfish of the skies revealed
To be a kiss of light the star
Which brings to our mutual palm the sleep of fullness
Pregnant in a first morning glance at day
Is ours alone and by no chance
The arm that holds the slightest breath
Has grown in golden blooms about the waist.

The taste of planets floats in the sound
The sight which feels the lightest touch
Does change into the finest aroma met
By thought or act of cell when the clouds drift
Through your eyes in soundless ecstasy and gasp
Held within the silken throat to stroke gentle soft
The heady air the speech of birds in talk
Which fires the stars, the suns of all our flames.

Edge

In prayer to the Earth,
In offering to root and rind,
In open modesty to warm breath of wind
And the unsuffering silence of growing branch,
The tall trunk of trees wanding air for day sun and light,
The axe leaves its splinters in gentle copse grass
And cares for nothing but sharp thought of grain.
Birds blink and move on.
Night comes to cut across the ringed Earth
In solemn arc of the closed lid...
Its deep edge is as palpable as the flesh of stars !

At The End Of A Day

Falling petal lost in Time's embrace
Float upon bright waters' race
Through grassy banks' guiding arms
Over smooth rocks to ocean's balms,
Wave-crests curving foamed and white,
To swirl and curl out of sight
Of land and beach; swim to rest
On vast sand floor's sea-grain breast.

Light water-swept fragile boat
Never ever again to float,
Barely touching, hardly there,
Spinning down through soft air
Of a Summer's sunset red,
From the hair of my beloved's head.

(Oh, my love, why stare forlorn?
The bloom still clings, though lightly worn!)

From A Distance

Blue of the heart the sky filled full
Yearn of distance
The dancing bird the heart
Spinning spinning in grace the sky
Face of the eye full to flow
To take the filling measure of my salt
Spun in blue the feather of her dress
The dancing heart the bird
Blue of the sky the heart filled full
Spinning spinning in grace of glance
Yearn of distance
The heart the sky the dance
Spinning spinning
To take in simple flow
This song
The simple sum and measure of my salt.

Somewhere In Silence

Water
And the Earth that has transmuted gold
Noble from density, gold uncorrupted of matter,
And the Earth that holds us,
The Earth-sired earth beneath the foot
The sand hot from the stars
Gathered by Time from space and the pace,
The tactile growth and shoot of it
Spun and sped in atom molecular
A vibrancy metallic...
And the Earth manifests real,
Pebbles in space and reels through,
The Earth that nurtures the hiding Treasure,
This pure Earth breathes
The systole and diastole breezes of the Old Gold Sea,
Waves deep emeralds in moonlight and the beach
Swims perfect beneath the stars,
Earth gold held solid within the vein rock heavy,
The Earth weighing nothing
Within the sharp Void, follows
A branching nature of things
And without need of a thought
Makes the Miracle,
Cradles the Marvellous in the highest of arms,
The quickest of hours,
And, seeing you emerge new from the ocean,
My eyes drink you in.
Pause.

Pause within the natural moment,
The moment that spawns all movement,
Its passage misted between time and event unfolding,
Ancient spiral of the heart rounding,
The Earth transformed of matter,
A gold that grows in quill-feathered veins
A liquid splendour;

The undulate of time
Spreads a mime danced from first to last,
Unbeginning,
Non-ending, formed of eternal event spontaneous
Leafs through earth-rooted reams,
Boles turned as pages under Millenniums' thumb,
And the Earth proud below the singing stars
Choirs within the silent Deep.

And somewhere in silence I found you
Between night and first light of dawns in splendour,
And somewhere and when you arise *ALIVE*
From the waters,
Poured wet with the anthracite sea
Your jet marble skin
Fired with a lattice phosphorescence
Runs with the suns of a Greater Sea,
Glows stellar cold fire to cover you
Naked beneath black jade skies;
Galaxies spiral on your coal-sooted flesh
And the Earth breathes the darkness in
Under carved ebony oceans
Spiked by gravity's lance in unseen magnetic
As the chiselled waters lap
Obsidian skin,
Their libation in grandeur of Nature's salt;
And your closed eyes are unopened cockleshells,
Your belly a night beach hiding a cave,
Your breasts conch a song that floods vast within you,
Sounding as sea-foam furling celestial
To *veena* in light from the stars
As the Earth yields its gold
To applaud you welcome,
To greet your primal steps from Our Sea;
And you let fall luminous pouring oceans
In a thin-starred waterfall profusion
To steep in infusion through fractal grains
Over the sands of your timeless tread

27

Never older than the one gilded moment
Between the gap in the vein
And the course of mute sap,
And the Earth poised at root
In thrall of the birthing moment vibrates
Where somewhere in silence you found me
Between the night and first light of dawns
Where the Earth sings beneath unending stars
Choired silences of the Deep.

Written

Scattered fragments of other men,
The lost poets,
Their cruel existence....
Broken memory traces,
Remnants of Beauty dancing,
Alone, spread like Shelley's corpse
On the beach of ignored, unwanted Evolution,
His stormy body whole, drowned,
His firefly spirit circling
Eyes so dead,
Eyes that once gleamed
With the Flame of Light:
Read his life pulsate on pages
Through a tempest night;
All that remains is *less...*
His sweet breath was more!

Scattered fragments of funeral pyres,
All that lives is dust and dies,
All that lived is scattered a-far
In the weave of ever-changing air,
Through the words of artists,
The lost poets,
The able men...
Their cruel existence.

Reading Below The Surface

Dark shadow images show,
Journey below
Thin skin
Surface, ripple
Free in jewel fragments...
Shapes in ormolu,
Filigree lace,
Patterns of New Tomorrows' face
Shimmer shiningly,
New as these moments
Place
Before your eyes
Words
As you read; and they grow,
Multiply....
Heed new-life glimmer
Like the bodies of snakes, gleam
Emerald wine, copper shimmering,
Noon-day sunlight stream;
They are not what they seem....
The Surface splits,
Shed snakeskin, undulating,
As an old year past
Or chrysalis cast
Aside, floats and flits
Conjunctiva thin....

The Inside
Quivers into life; fish
Leap clear
From downstream element, veer
And splash and swish,
Sparkling patterns,
Mercurial passions....
This new growth pushes
On, strong and adamantine;
Rich psychedelic bushes,

Flowers, into action
While the Surface drops
Away from the pace and pulse:
The blossoming never stops,
Creates this day
New shores' impulse
As never before...
And the Surface sloughs
Away.

Iridescent butterflies
Spread silk wing
Glistening peacock eyes,
Dance majestic, light,
Beating air of vibrant dawns,
Stand tremble-new as new-born fawns,
Delicate, as if white
Snowflakes
Fall soft through jet-black night,
As with tender-tongue-touch of snakes
These life-rhythms grow
Away from jettisoned Surface below,
Quick to ferment (and brew),
Solidify in text,
Move to this very next (a-new)
As web Surface bubbles below,
Heaves with the birth of a thought,
Cleaves by its own gem-light
And split-second age;
Its form is caught upon a page....
Brief life, in splendour, dies,
And the Surface curls below
Where dark shadow
Images show
Us their closed Eyes....

The Desert

One's weaknesses yield an inmost sorrow,
Though none is greater than No Tomorrow!

30

Booming Of The Day

Pearl of shoe and hill of horn,
Waxen bell from trumpets torn,
Flower of wood from bedrock born
Through the booming of the day.

Bride of bush and cave of thorn,
Net of veil from thunder's scorn,
Gem of mud from jewel sawn
Through the booming of the day.

Bevel of sphere and side of dawn,
Face of fell from epochs worn,
Grin of hood from valley's yawn
Through the booming of the day.

Slice of salt and tear of faun,
Ring of shoot from seaweed lawn,
Drive of mood from cello's brawn
Through the booming of the day!

In Dreams Yet To Come

Go with me
In my dream
Down riverbank,
Through swirling stream,
Fly through air,
Swim through sea,
For in dreams
We will ever be,
So in dreams yet to come,
Vade-mecam,
Vade-mecam,
O in my dreams
Go with me,
Go with me....

The Orange Sections Of The Sun

The orange sections of the sun
Close up gradual as the slope
Cloud mounts its black overhang
Roofing the bay;
A storm tilts in to its cup.

Gulls soar white against the deep
Grey gills of ocean breathing
In before it sinks
Beneath rain and the cloak
Swirled by a night with no stars.

Heightened only by the screams
That rip the waves,
That decorate thin the rush
Air drawn down
A sanded throat of stones,
The crash of dawn light
Heard before it breaks
The thin skin a-top the sea
Shows the surface of all
In colour of salt's snap moment sharp,
In taste of sweet seaweed aeons alive,
Echoes over waiting beaches
Wet in silent smiles of shells,
The newest dreams of ancient fishes
Swim to meet the solid cliff
And are born in the songs of grasses
That laze and stir in idle winds above.

Quickie

The moment of surprise
Passes to form *O!*
Can you believe!
It? *No!* You shouldn't!
Really?
O how... how.... *Unexpected...!*

As Seeds Scout

Sending a seed-scout out ahead,
Lightning grows as cranes fly,
As streams flow to rivers,
As fish swim seas,
As lanes form,
As trees fork the air,
As thoughts move,
As flames fire up,
As snakes thrust,
As roots snake,
Sending a seed-scout out ahead....

An Unknown Time

I spent an unknown time
In a mystic place
Without
The bird and the fish
And the man in between.

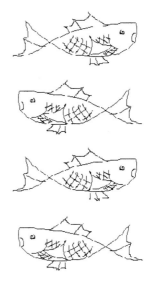

I spent an original time
In a younger face
Within
The bird and the fish
And the man in between.

I spent an eternal time
At a deeper pace
With
The bird and the fish
And the man in between.

The brightest night
About me laced
The bird and the fish
And the man in between.

33

The Sibilant Cell

Tendril of gene the sibilant cell,
Circle of growing to chromosome push,
Drive of knowing the turning wheel,
Tune of sinew the willowing gush.

Forces that draw the droning clamp
Channel syzygy by polaric lamp,
Lumen of spray the pollenous damp,
Fire of magma the modular stone.

Listening silences
Within wood
Hover in senses
From root to hood.

Breath of molecule the harmonic hive,
Swarm to corpuscle the gathering bone,
Curl of feather to soaring dive,
Moisture of movement the mirroring hone.

And meadows simmer soft
Beneath swing of stars aloft.

Spread of constriction the running line,
Repeat of pattern the curving clone,
Strength of manner the climbing sine,
Rumble of resting sheer stemming done.

Oceans in splendour
By light of the moon
Where beaches harbour
Lost splinters of noon.

Sun

Topaz climbing sun
Spread your light upon
Us,
Bathe your heat over us,
Warm and bronze us,
Supple limb us,
Cover us in radiance,
In breeze balm,
Hold us in your sightless sight,
Mould us flaming sun, dance
In your cloud-burned palm,
Your fiery fingers askance,
Wide your far-flung arm
And rest us
Gentle, gentle sun,
Upon your rocking dun
And oven-roasted earth
So that we may feel your girth
To glow in sleep
Within your orbit brave,
Paved seconds on the booming deep,
So we may close our window,
Close the skin-thin veil to minnow,
To willow, to rave,
To dream the hidden force of stars!

Star Gothic

See the rats at run
Pockmarked over curl-tooth moon,
The ancient scream as wonder held
In ice surprise
Against the patter-footed stars,
Open within scrape-claw deeps
The rat-tail comets spun
To pull the spring and set
The one wire we all await.

35

In Painted Silence

Within
The magnet gaze of lovers
Flicks a flame,
Circles a line invisible,
Engraves a name
Deep set in painted silence
Breathed infinite to ring
An unseen breadth of bells
Within
Vasting temples of the heart....

In Search Of Temples

Beneath the brow the beaten tread
Falls constant to the throb of heart,
Under the bough the trodden track
Lays waiting in the shape of paths
To temples caressed by moon.

Under the leaf the curling vein
Branches gossamer by cell unseen,
Beneath the turf the crawling root,
Spirals lean shoots green in search
Of temples caressed by moon.

Beneath the sky the sun-dipped wing
Soars a wonder won by web of feather,
Under the cloud the released drop
Falls to land a billionth time dropt
On temple roofs caressed by moon
...*Light!*

36

Great Age Turns

Great Age turns its face to me,
A pterodactyl in every pore,
And with eyes that deep swim a primal sea,
Stares straight to my very core.

Primordial forest streaks its long lank hair,
The first cell sleeks its beard,
Its mouth a cave, some creature's lair,
Dark-breathes a sound which every soul has feared!

Great Age turns its fixed face to me,
A trilobite in each primeval pore,
Beckons all souls their bones to flee,
Its scars, its stars, its epochs to explore!

So when it's time to leave this place,
To join with All that's Past,
Look Great Age firmly in its ancient, pockmarked face,
When you bravely breath your last!

And should you chance to meet me,
Beyond that time-locked, final slam-shut Door,
Look close to skin and surprise to see
A pterodactyl in every pore!

Thumbing Through

Lips of Imagination
Construct each thought, each nation,
Kiss the passing ages,
Words on fleeting pages
Bound in books unprinted,
Unprintable, because
That which *Is* (although able)
Soon fades to *Never Was*....

Under that final cover
Time takes Absence for a lover.

37

The Dry Man

A hold is lost over me.
The Darkness has to bathe
In lack of water where the Dry Man
Walks, awaits
Fattening of shadows,
Shortening of heights,
The movement of airs across breathing waters,
Breadth of heavens.

The Dry Man sits,
Heels on hanks,
Arms winged,
Wings folded,
Beneath
The follicle of Life,
Between
Time and event
Unblinking.
From the first
His thirst
Clasps me not.
A way is lost to water:
His bones flake.

A hold is lost through the Sea.
The Great Dark has to bathe
In lack of tears
Where the Dry Man weeps waterless
To wait,
His sliding sands unslaked,
Depth of dusts,
Moments of movements
Across the still Deeps.

Great Ocean you are mine.
The Dry Man has me not
Within his lemon Past.
Great Ocean, you are mine,
For now, you are *mine....*

38

Star-fire From The Hat

Star-fire in cricket song
Picked out in light,
Each raging furnace calm
Ancient insect pattern,
Mute swarm throating
Through staggering depths
In royal slow turn,
Chitinous pulse and thrum
Upon stilled air warm and wonderful,
Poise the living stars.

The Plough sheer upon horizon rests,
Spoons planet rocks to early-bird
A premature breakfast, while wormless
Space parts in effortless gift,
Lets wormed Earth shoot through
In wingless path to fly
The feathered deep black crystal,
Where, buffeted bright by unseen winds
Echo radiant insect songs
In chirrup here in this world of stones.

I love to hear crickets' chorus on a star-breathed night
Rise in the air to fall and disappear
Within the timeless globes within the wind
Which are the souls of stars,
Long since gone although deathless living
Between clouds of stellar dust,
Among the flickering thought of them,
Rarely achieved
Until a night as this one, invisible
Pulls the rabbit from its black crown
To lilt of insect orchestra,
Pivot of experience,
Pilot to the soul.

In Memory Of Them

Utilise damp green,
Wrap it in prism swathe
And hurl it to the night
In memory of Picasso, Magritte, Toyens.

Take lemon yellow hot,
Cover it in sunbeams
And hurl it to infinity
In memory of Brancusi, Matta, Gorky.

Select a sliver of glass,
Bury it in moonbeams full
And hurl it to the Milky Way
In memory of Duchamp, Arp, Bellmer.

Use self-reflection;
Carry on in this way until the memory
Of all people truly worthy
Has been honoured.

Only then choose your *own*
Object
And hurl it into the rest of your life
In your own memory....

(Or, in flourish of final arrogance, just eat a tomato!)...

A Winter's Summer Spring

The chill winds of Winter
First are felt on August nights
When the warm full-moon rages
Silent on the Deep.

And in the coldest brittle dip,
Where Winter rests a December head,
Nests that full and future egg
The arousing bud of Spring!

You Turn Your Eyes

Creamed thought of albino caves
The foreshortened pearls
Tumble curved the skin silk of neck
Arched in hold of head
Rapt within magnificence magnetic
A spiral limb of cells
Around the ecstatic centre
In thrall of living grace
Alert the steady gaze toward
Torn label moon
Riding the space above hills rounded
By time and the flowing
Seasons in their vigilance
A violent peace of transmutation
A change of thunderous calm
The still lake in silent upheaval
The breathless sands orgasmic ripple
The solid rock diffuse in steam
Rising as moisture prismatic
In your compacted sight of dark feathers
Cyclops' singular stare into eyes
Returning the essence of being
A creature of Earth alert
The same, in depth, as me...
A meeting of *presence*
A feeling of *worlds*....

Under The Orbiting Top

Ocean spins its wheels,
Whips pewter veins,
Wintering, whistling, whimpering.

Glacial clouds topple a hiss of elements
Dipped in lead, a call for furnace fire
Under the orbiting top.

41

Time In Wonder

Time,
Behind this gated wonder,
Leaves the leaves the wood the tree,
Steps out beyond itself,
Looks back to the shadowed wheel
All turning stopped,
Cropped short and sullen whisper
Echo of a next moment near begun,
Gazes all around to ponder nature,
Hesitates, sniffs stillness in the air,
Drives a sudden rim
To start again in motion forward...
Here comes the rain!

Time,
The leaking wonder,
Gift of motion the great consumer,
Marries to event,
Breath of Universal lung
Ceases never,
Ever constant never even,
Takes a tickle in the vein,
Pumps a curved and covered rib,
Laughs a gallon
Bubbling in murmur of waterfalls
While water falls
Until it stops... here comes the sun
Shining over tops of trees!

Time,
The gifted, giving wonder,
Never pulls, always pulls,
The patterned carpet out from under,
Fells the tree in haste
To grow another in the very place
Of second's tock, minutes ticking,
Mountain's silence deep is thinking
Cloud's steady hour,
Clock's relentless pace

Shredding days into nights,
Movement unaware is sleeping
Below its own face...
Here comes the moon
Orbing over half-moon eyelids half-closed!

Time,
The warrior, wounded wonder,
Hero of the phoenix hour,
Grasps at clouds to fall
Its foot-stepped days in easier drift,
Slides down rainbows,
Surrounds itself in mist,
Mounts the gale
To ride out the storm
Powered by lightning thrusts,
Delivers the accurate instant
Here within the twilight realm
Where smile meets tear,
Where fire meets ice to mingle,
To take furnace heart out of the sun...
Here comes an early snow
And Winter not yet begun!

Time,
The lovers' mislaid wonder,
Steals a kiss soft as a wish of water
Carried by the fickle breeze
Made by silent feather,
Wings through a waving spread of trees,
The arms of lovers
Greeting from afar,
Their foot-falls counting unknown measure,
Hearts in rhymed unreason
Under rise and fall of chest and skin,
The moment slowed; their sight
Alone touches until voices
Mix and laugh to shout...
Here comes the single dawn
Which All Time in its haste left out!

43

Amber's Song

The deep-sucked roots tell
The silvered leaves
Of stars that gracious fell
To glimmer bright the blades,
The ancestral grass fresh flowing
Through meadow soft and glades
Mellow-dewed with all
The tumbled tears of nightfall,
Special in the awning dark.

O hark! all souls to the sound,
The soaring flight of heightening space... O hark!
A bounding, boundless song ethereal
Ripples the living earth
And bubbles songs of constellations
Over listening pastures browsing
Upon the star-creamed food,
O harken! Harken to the earthing stellar brood!

Look! Look there... a star within a flower bell
Cellos in vibrato,
Leaves play the choirs of furthest suns
To pitch wild in the black pitch dark...
O hark! O hark; can you tell?
My soul is growing,
My soul is growing,
I grow as sure as night is sowing stars
By mystic blissfulness
And an inner brightness glows
Upon a sleeping land
To grace mine eyes, my face,
My joy-spun teary sight,
As stars dance soft upon my haloed hand
Within this most glorious of nights,
And I become of ecstasy
Formed of every cell
A glowing, a glowing....

I am Amber, I am Amber, Amber of the Stars!
O stars suck up through buttercups,
Sparkle upon my breasts,
And by their light but alien touch
My very breasts caress....
O never could I guess
That as all slept the stars come down to spark
Afloat and bright
To comb the hills' night hair,
To plough the fields the earth to test
As if to sense the round depth of it,
Shimmer long within
The glimmer-long fronds of ripening wheat
And star-dance shining spheres of feet
To whisk and wisp the air
In pleasantry and peace.

O see them, see them glowing there,
How they happy light the spindle trees,
How they tingle through the grasses to amuse
Each hiding mouse and vole,
Each silent-staring cow bemused,
Transfix the earth-blinded mole!
O how soft the stars run upon my arm
And kiss my sleep-shorn face,
My curves of thighs
With fragile touch of butterflies!
O Magick! O Joy! O Bliss!
O lack of harm!
Can there be any place
As wonderful, as beautiful
In proper thrall as this?
But... Oh! what happens, my fey luminosities?
Be not afraid, be not afraid of me,
For I am simply so
As all may plainly see...
They go! They go... O my! the stars displace,
Go to float aloft! Why so? Why so?
Look! They quick retreat to shield the lightening sky,

45

To stud the shawl of night
With their myriad eye,
Returned from whence they fell!
I inward yell
And cry
O My Soul! They rise, my grace-tuned stars!
See how they stellar rush
Up the plush of velvet air
With the distal sound of cellos, *veenas*, sitars!
They shake, they quake...
The Dark One must have bade them there;
They must leave, so that sprite
Should not come near
To work in sinister spite,
Yes! It's *he* they fear!

My dance of stars has gone.
O now I am left
Alone,
Bereft,
To treasure precious thoughts of my dear
Stars that traverse space and travel time...
But yet I'm Amber, I am Amber,
I am she whose soul is growing,
My soul is growing,
My soul is growing,
I am Amber of the Stars!
Amber of the Stars!

In The Nucleus

In the nucleus, there the sap
Slithers and as a magnet draws,
Coils a vital course,
Twists humming in the heated lap,
Drums the bone,
Taps the root,
Returns itself, primed, to the One,
And, *laughing*, grows a shoot....

With Her At My Dark Side

With her at my dark side
I laugh and jest with the teeming stars,
Eat moon-pie, magpied moonbeams,
Smile comet-tailed float-ember curls,
Meteor my mind and fling the sun
To cross the unmetred mote-mile vault,
Cry in astrodomed astrolabe tears
Wide joy unfaulted,
Star-creamed of milky space-fruit whey,
Of sun-dust, of joy-tide dreamed delights
And feather-bone, head thought-hurling flights,
Pillow-giggle fights in long-limbed nights
Of intimacy, silence entwined, moist
Crow-cock dawns and wet moonsets
With her at my dark side.

With her at my dark side,
Morning arrows new-bright slow and glimmer-glimpsy,
Opens slomo-misty its thirsty, seeing, seeking eye;
And as her skin curves tactile over backlit gypsy dales,
At first steady-light, all is poised
Upon a precipice, stone-quiet,
Only hearts beating breath's breathing sighs,
And thighs
The dawn in, all heavy-lidded birds caught out,
Outside,
Mulled within the hairs of early lull;
The follicles of fields fondle the hided,
Whited boughs of hidden scythes;
While blood leaps charged through trout-veined vales,
Smooth kidney rocks voiceless warm the swimming sap
And all future times and chimes are lampblack
Lain in earth-gland lap,
With her at my dark side.

47

With her at my dark side,
The sizzling solar sun-grill thrills the steep,
Scales Sleep's deep-sight sphere
Within her eggshell-peeped Eye,
Wide world wide-awakes,
Woken; slumber broken by the quakes
Of a dream-away dream slipping
Under in lumbering, stirring slide,
As flesh fibres tense to tone unseen, all past forgotten,
The present conjures to steal the living moment,
Nostrils sun-flare the final dips of night out...
They flip inside out, never to return a snore to lip,
Nor retrace to severed seas to hide
Where salts of fishes freeze slivered silver shores to
Purring jungles, brimmed, untrimmed full-leaf dank
In parrot-fashioned trees,
In flashing, thunder-ember eyes of skulking,
Shank-hunting hunger,
As I kiss, unearthed mud-nerved lips
In day-bliss pale and pout,
With her at my dark side.

With her at my dark side,
Day dives its hard mud into driving streamered dreams,
Wheeled loins root-throb a tunnelled trunk
And stem-dark vein, volcanoes tumble tremors,
Tremble abraxas in the one bone,
Dream's aquarium dunks legend-dry into lovers' clover,
Settles to abide In peace, in quieted organic cell,
No rumble fish slant angry,
Shell-shocked from sea-floor
Docks of weed-frond bone-marrow caves,
Saline in lifeline, blood sand-sweat of pulling ocean's
Effort, but rest, within eternal sea-chest
Breast-cribs of tubing waves,
Which, incessant, pour and run through tidal race
Of corpuscle, in the naked, polished jet-stone black
Ivory-caged and golden-ribbed vault,
Under the sing-song swathes of sun-hid missal

Of living stars, of lifing pulse,
Of giving life and love
With her at my dark side.

With her at my dark side,
I astride the whisper-wishing trees
Which swish and glide green,
Await the eagle wings of myths
To ride in purpled careen,
With her at my dark side.

The Moon Nests

The moon nests
Upon luminous clouds and softs
The night and its closing dark
With a breath of dreams
Glimpsed through watered milk
And the eyelashes of a floated sleep.

Glide and step light
The tender arch in poise and air...
There you dance in gentle swirl,
Kissed glow of moonlight skin
Enthralling the tranced eyes
Of stilled trees and serving grass,
Radiant within the warm and cradled air
Under a sweep of jewels,
Stars gathered to the moment
In witness to beauty beatific in grace,
Movement of living clouds
Limbed fine and long,
Your body's buoyant gesture,
Here, where the crickets sing
Around your vibrant heart and where
The moon nests....

Elusive The Shadow

Elusive the shadow,
Ephemeral the thought,
Dream-foot dreams run and flow
To the Endless Ocean, caught
Below, dark and dimmed,
Until the dreamer wakes
On wings of brimmed
Light anewed to fresh
The Eye, and shakes
Away sleep's undulations meek;
Hidden Sea's salting mesh
Brines the morning beak!

A stumbled course and day seems drab,
Ordinary, mundane and crabbed
In the weaving weft of plodding motions,
No magic touches leaf, no hill-crests blush,
The sun remains just sun,
No zest moves within the breast,
No inspirational emotions,
The Earth is still, unbegun,
No spin, the climbing clouds just climb,
The day the day, the sky the sky,
Unfelt blows dry winds' rush,
Unthought Time,
Beauty unseen, unfound;
Meaning makes no move, no sound....

Spawned and doffed with a grace unheard
Comes *charged* the spark,
Voluminous fills the air,
Birding to polish all in its own mystic sap,
Jumps all vision sharp to the Eye,
Thrills the vital earth and taps the rooted lap,
Shines each scene and sound,
All fragrance, each lacing vein,
And rounds all within a central majesty,

Flings inner doors wide to gape and gain;
So, as Time comes and goes,
Drink every Marvellous Moment, and see
In a draught as deep as time is dear,
That, bottomless, the well brims with waters clear,
All too soon it overflows
And pours as sand
Down all the years....

The Tumbled Trail

Each stone unique, the tumbled trail
Turns to round the wetted vale,
Loops a padded earthy bake
To circumnavigate dank marsh and lake
In solitary persistence.

Aside the creek, the tumbled trail
Curves out from the wetted dale,
Snakes a warm dun path of old
To thread bluebell trees a zigzag bold
In solitary persistence.

Tint earth teak, the tumbled trail
Leaves leaf and wood the sky to sail,
Climbs the short-grass whispered hill
To up and up through rough ruck rock and rill
In solitary persistence.

Birds to seek, the tumbled trail
Scales scarp and scrub to wag its tail,
Fringed by wind-seared brake and thyme
It sparsely lines a cloud-search mime
In solitary persistence.

At high peak, the tumbled trail
Turns to round dry hill's avail,
Scraping sky in humpbacked exalt,
Firm to endure hard element assault
In solitary persistence.

51

The Fallow Fields

The stars are come down to the fallow fields,
Spread firefly across the bowed wet grass,
Hang in suspense over the milding meadows,
Touch low and light to sprinkle
The hedged field shields
Which lose to black their lush damp-green sap
Corming into Autumn, as the stars fascinate the land
Through nighttime.

The stars are new come down to the fallow fields,
Skim tree-top lattice and leafing bush
To spark alive the veins of plants,
And, lit pale by the setted moon, the collected nimbus
Limbs of luminous clouds push up eldritch
From an horizon deeper black than sky
Like shark fins white
Cutting through the under to plough dark-rich
The living oceans of trees, their snakeskin souls
In search of calmer seas, and everywhere around
The stone-held silence sounds the silent sounds
Of stealth and sleeping life that hovers
Through nighttime.

The stars are fresh come down to the fallow fields,
Play night-sky across the breathing ground
As I lie here listening in the dark, dark dark
And think of her,
The way the sky sings in her hair,
The sunrise flashes from her eyes,
How her skin reflects star-glow
And her warm breath mists dawn windowpanes,
A new day crisp and clear and dear
Having found its way; and I turn
To gaze over the dream-dark earthy gentle land
Within a midnight mystery
As planets dance between moist grass blades bowing

In the fallow fields a-glow,
Where the stars dust their ray-spun snow
To weave the souls of plants a-sewing
In cobweb lace of leaves
Through nighttime.

And I Am Happy In My Sleep

And I am happy in my sleep, heaped and flying,
Both, in splendid reverie
Zoom in and out...
And am merry in my earth, boxed and booming,
Both, to onward float an ancient Sea,
Great age steeped in *kalpas'* mystery!

And I sprite athletic in my shroud, still and soaring,
Both, full-sail proud,
I sing! I shout!
And dart strong in my crowd tomb, bone and wing,
Both, lain within a roomless room
Of windows made in open star-full fling!

And I laugh living in my dream, locked and free,
Both, the sky the skull I won,
Scale its skin
And clap in mirth within my pit, fixed and roaming,
Both, for I can lace around the round-bell Earth
With wising motion of a moon!

And I, space-walking in my glee, weight and none,
Both, the stars caress...
I don their shift of frost and soot
And sing racy in the Absolute, time and not,
Both, for my demise is but a deathless death,
A seed waits sure on primal growth of root!

Related In Light: (The Pointy Stars)

Related in light,
They forge a link, though, don't they,
The pointy stars?
They play their part versus
The ballooning action of parting ways,
Blink milky, flirt to entrance us,
And as did highwaymen of old, waylay
The cobbling sleigh, the treasured coach
Of night-wing with their sparkling eye,
Spark sled-slow to stir its late pitchblende,
Twitch their shooting flares down
To darkest end, where day reaches to encroach
And make silken grand an entrance,
Flourish of dawn's yawning cape
Through horizon's earthbound wings!

Lift your head and stand to gape
As the shard sky delivers diverse
Uncountable luminosities,
Watch them level and shoot their fire down
From malt and peppered zenith crown,
Image through the unleapt ditch,
Nudge and turn the stellar-patterned dish,
Clustered as streetlights of the next town
Seen from a stone-throw distance;
And do they hold on high the hard
Diamond lights of alien cities?
Look... there they beckoning are,
See them wink through the smoked scales
Of scudding mackerel skies,
Without a reckoning care or sense
For all we know... but hear their cries!
O if you had the impossible chance,
Wouldn't you just love to fin and go,
Rocket up to the very socket
Of the eyeing sky, and, without a backward glance,

Explore locked and weirding lands,
Paving airless moat from star-foot
To shake their star-souled hands?

Without peer or par
The simple star coverlet, night's ears,
Birthed of the same vast mother... hark!
They jet along in the jet above, light years
From us and one another,
Radiant they burn, bring light to dark,
Wave as strangers might,
Related in light.

Wood At Nightfall

I stand in a wood that ignores me,
Pretends I'm not here staring at treetops
In the wind, at tumult of leaf,
At twist of old branch,
While the trees paint a green mood
On the wet sides of hills.

The solid air carries
Their sound to the sea
Across meadows which listen
In timeless intent.

The trees whinny as the hedges cluck
Clattering in the soft earth air,
On this demanded day
All full of tree-bark
And the dying strains of epochs
Cut free of the clock.

This wood only cares for each season
And the absence of time.
Tree roots whisper rippling
Below as I take my leave,
Only no-one notices,
Least of all this wood at nightfall!

Vampire

You, too, know me my sweet, the wings
That bore Antigone aloft also spin
Me to heights which crumbled turrets sense
But do not look above, the wings
Which leathern fly and flit between shadows now
Melt and seep through the weave, the cloth of Time
And Timelessness spent waiting for the sap of tombs
Rent asunder by grief and the foul departed, the wings
They bear upon bare shoulders, doff a spirited air
More dense than shadows, than lead,
Than the heart of the murdered ones,
Heavier than the club, the two-handled sword,
The gryphon's tooth, falls the gentle kiss
Upon the dappled throat, the wings
Concealing, landscape sucked dry
Upon the hidden sigh,
Breath of ancient leather and pulse of the crushed ruby,
Wet as the fur of this animal clutched now to breast,
The growl, eerie low and menace rumble, toothed
Stumble, the wings
Hiding in shade of the vein voided,
Split and slashed asunder
By the essence of enamel dream and nightmare,
Down that sorrowed crack in time and meaning,
Falling to the quickened second
Buried in the bone, the wings
Having beat a long last moment
In sapped shadow of the cell....

The body numbed arisen, false phoenix, the wings
Folded within muscle embalmed and bitten
Lovingly in the silk thought,
Wrapped in cocoon of infinite chloroform
To walk in cloistered gothic,
Buried in that dulled sound
Of the waterfall of stars, the wings

56

Heard in the clicking of embers,
In the haemoglobin musty with spores,
He the haemogoblin who runs
To rot through your corridors,
You the dancer of the horn-footed waltz
Fusty with those ancient doors
That never open onto scenes of coffined tendernesses,
Blood flowers of fortune,
Forgetfulness breathed in through nostrils
Which do not pretend of decay,
The once-desiring nerve now
Quenched of ache, the wings
Concealed within the brain, all thought folded,
Staked in limbic aspic, moronic brain-cell,
Limping ghost inside each floating urge,
And the eyes of consciousness
In their myriad swirl clamped shut
By that putrid drip and act, the wings
Closed within another's torn and shredded heart
Of claws, the vein in limbo a mist upon a windowpane,
Pain of aborted delivery,
The screaming murmur,
The shouted mumble,
The howling silence,
Sound of the ripped cloth
From off the corpse's face, the wings
Snapped,
Torn from the hovering soul,
Gone forever, vanished
In slow ritual of funereal haste,
Deep pang of sorrow,
Thinned blood of hopeless desire
Trickles down the weeping jowl,
Pools to vapour at the feet
Where trample trashed those fans of life,
The wings....

Water From The Living Well

Take an open cup and sup gentle,
From the base-point stir it up and gentle,
The crystal liquid innermost elemental
Spring and fountainhead in constant swell,
The ever-present, omnipotent, silent and archetypal
Water from the living well.

Take open lips and sup it up but gentle,
Pour it single-handed to the source replenished subtle,
Tap the innermost crystal liquid elemental,
Swell spring and fountainhead in closest spell,
The eternal flow shining archetypal
Water from the living well.

Egg Of Stars

Salt spray of fishes fly
Off the sea, polished flying fishes
Leap to try and reach
Night skies of ebony
Beyond moon beach
Beneath the Egg of Stars
On high.

Salt spray of fishes flies
In the wind
As each swishing flying fish tries
To find substance real of sky,
To breathe the stars' breath
Leaping beyond the fond
Beach-break waves beneath
The Egg of Stars that paves,
Silent, on high.

Alien ether,
Alien nether,
Foamed other,
O Egg of Stars!

Lustred Egg of Stars!
Your filaments shell above
In fundamental essence
Affirmed to firmament expanse
And fixed to zenith point in time
By crucifixion of orbit's girth,
By virtue of sparkled spins
And void flown wide above,
On high.

O Egg of Stars! How I constant
Love your wheel, your crown,
Your slow and steady reel,
Your unheard sigh,
The mewling solar winds...
O how your myriad luminosities
Await a fractal birth!

O Egg of Stars, O tears of Emptiness!
Joyous are your dusts of night,
When clocks have scented suns
Within the longing eyes of fishes,
As fishes fly to cradle stars silent,
On high.

Beneath The Dog-rose

Beneath
The dog-rose the blind road,
Whipped veil dragging under,
Petal sharpened the flower blade
Strikes a rock asunder,
Slices sentences askance
Words spinning,
Crazy dance,
Pull the tab,
Release the prong white fang
Ivory page
Laid out for words to hang,
Almost neat.

Street Of Dreams

Crystallised flowers on the Street of Dreams,
What's in a moment on the Street of Dreams?
Ebony pathways through the Street of Dreams,
Jade circles in the Street of Dreams,
Nothing's ever really what it seems
On the Street of Dreams.

Ghosts float slow on the Street of Dreams,
Gliding lace unseen on the Street of Dreams,
Clocks rain down on the Street of Dreams,
Neon thunder rolls on the Street of Dreams,
Everything's really what it seems
On the Street of Dreams.

In the dreaming ways
Iron railings bloom in new *fleur-de-lis*,
Pianos pick their pinto keys,
Armchairs huddle up to
Pavement squares,
Withdraw their feet to
Shield them from the passing cars,
Spectres in the Street of Dreams,
Oceans in the Street of Dreams,
Anteaters in the Street of Dreams.

In the Street of Dreams
Beds sleep under canopies,
Moonbeams shine out silver greys
Translucent on the Street of Dreams,
Opal mists upon the Street of Dreams,
Snow feathers on the Street of Dreams,
Crystal mornings on the Street of Dreams.

Tight shadows,
Black shadows,
White shadows
On the Street of Dreams.

Cars stopped,
Night stopped,
Time stopped
On the Street of Dreams,
People sleeping,
Time tock-ticking,
Tarmac snoring
On the Street of Dreams
All futures seem
Empty fragrances spiralling
In smoke of a rare pale green
Flying through the Street of Dreams,
Reeling on the Street of Dreams,
Ruck rocking on the Street of Dreams.

The Street of Dreams grows from crystal flowers,
What's in a moment on the Street of Dreams?
Ebony circles,
Jade pathways,
Neon thunder
Over and under,
Nothing's ever really what it seems
On the Street of Dreams!
Beds snoring,
Ghosts foaming,
Oceans floating,
Everything's just what it seems
On the Street of Dreams.

Strange footsteps on the Street of Dreams,
Sleepwalking on the Street of Dreams,
Armadillos on the Street of Dreams,
Tall shadows on the Street of Dreams,
And I'm flying on the Street of Dreams,
Only in my dreams,
In my dream
I'll meet you on the Street of Dreams,
In my dreams on the Street of Dreams,
O in my dreams....

Forever Cove: (Your Dream Is Over)

O John, O John, you're gone, you're gone...
Through purple mists of satin air,
Over silver lattice of smoke-wreathed nights,
Over gold-holed clouds that sing despair,
Into earth shell ochre dreams of flesh-fold delights,
Your spectre's mesh
Moves to the fresh sounds of birds,
To lightning winds of rushing ways,
Embalmed in black coral beach displays,
In time-lost joys and jagged flint dismays,
Of psychedelic rainbowed breeze-blown dawns
That last for resounding vast
Eternity, spun
Freeze-framed and finely drawn
Against a gold-fanned, famed sunrise
As your sudden past, lost and done
In final life-stare shines jewel breath,
And sets in death
Behind rich-lived roads of All Days' eyes,
With mirrored Mind
And Being's stone
Stilled within the facet-flame
Of your glowing body's hearth; unsung
Songs flow into reddened earth,
And suns of days yet to come, drift
In a distant future dark,
Go to blow and spark
Full-sailed spindrift
Riffs and raves,
Or golden tunes that chorus and call us
To comb and love
Beneath deep-space stars above,
And move as One, together,
With the lilt of Forever Cove's
Changing ocean spume-salt waves,
As you leave the fang-tooth walrus tusk

Of a bullet-broken husk
Wounded, weeping, rolled upon
The seeping clock of jiving, funky art,
Of Time's long-bled bed
Rock
Of living song, of Heart,
From which you have, for now, to part...
O John, O John, you're gone, you're gone,
O John, O John,
You're *gone....*

Epitaph

I've just gone around a corner
Out of sight.
You may see me,
Meet with me, one day....

Well, you might...!

So until then I merely say
HEY! *I'm just around a corner...*
Out of sight....

At Monkstone Point, 3am. *(In My London Bed)*

Here where the waters blow wet in breezes
Beneath these age-skinned monoliths
To coat in balm of salt their blind stone stares
In spray of night-seasoned mists
The headland thrusts
Tree and tree and tree and tree
Against a crowded black low cover and clouded,
Each veil sibilant in poised solicitude
Signs of heartwood thought
A natural meditation
Upon some silent centre.

63

Long Shadows

The day has drawn itself in long shadows
Extended its mythic bones fingering grasses
Hair on the head of fields where rivers run
The loping gait of water over stones reflecting cloud
Soon to be fluid mirrors to the murmuration of stars
The owl's wing is my silent contemplation
In hush of dark.

Talk to me not of tenderness the heart
Holds such an ache as would sire
Beings shaped in silver tremblings
To scatter over the night earth
Their pearled forms as raindrops fled before a storm
Breaks in deep rich rumble the lining of worlds
The undelivered yearning of the soul.

Talk not to me of tenderness the skin
Sings from its cells the Siren's searchlight song
A beacon made of a music lost within the substance
The stone the air the tree the tangle of the world
Alien matter which shreds feeling
And hands it to the winds
Yet is replaced as from a tireless well that sits within.

The day has shadowed itself in long drawings
Extended its finger bones of grassy myth
Hair on the heads of rivers where fields run
The stone gait of cloud reflecting the water
Murmuration of mirrors to the fluid stars
The owl's hush is my winged contemplation
In dark of silence.

Talk not to me of tenderness
The heart holds wings.

The Nightside of Truth

On the nightside of truth
Freedom comes in glide of silence
Darkened wings
To roof over grained fields
In mute conspiracy with deaf sky,
The secret trees and howling forests,
The ticking wood and bowling hours,
The seasoned hand and bucking plough,
Scattered insect the midnight earth
Where lurks the wolf of Innocence,
The cow of death and luckless leaf
Spinning in the wind and aimless
Parallel to the great sun's ghost,
The talking hill and random-folded land.

Wide is the never-ended stream and burning sea,
Tall as mountains the trodden soil tumbling,
Rich is the rain and wealthy the rainbow
That never fades from around a never-setting star,
Star of crumbling rock and blown sand whistling,
Touch the hewn stone at the stream head mumbling
Of kings and the torn hour of peace and calm storm,
Fade the fine Winter on the sleek cheek of grace
And cup the rough hand around fallen petal,
The used gland of Spring
Quieted to the harsh lullaby of rooks
In the topmost branches of the Years' long hair.

To lie for to gaze in wonder
At the up of the sky its limbs flowing
Horizontal and huge a billowing glory globe,
To run through the strands of the sea-wet oceans
In effort of dripping glass the rain-soaked High Way,
To cup the first thought on the nightside of truth.

Remember Life: (This You Can Do For Me)

When tubing blood has taken flight,
When the cell lies silent in the vein
Way beyond any daying search of night
To pump and jive, abandoned, without gain
Of breath that, living, ran upon the constant
Jump of vibrant tread,
Rising to the swell of life which issued from the sea...
Yes, when I am dead,
This you can do for me...
Bequeath my True Being
To hiss of wave,
To atom molecular galaxies hidden within,
To frost of stars that spark cold fire
And myriad roof to midnight pave,
And I shall will my light
To first hint of sun dawns,
The primal glow which heralds 'All Again Begin'....

Blood of the ocean,
Flesh of the earth,
Skeletal stone,
Orbital girth,
The song of the wind,
Equator and south,
All drop behind
When spirit sweeps timeless
From our empty Mouth!

I shall commit my essence
To the pulse in that blood,
To its emerald fires, its leaves,
Its pace and its flood,
To the Universal Name and its Absolute Sense,
To the laugh in the sigh,
To the sigh in the laugh,
To the living face which all creatures own,
When I take my leave and leave home,
Yes, when I am dead, no more to earthly roam

All these will fall behind
As I sweep through stars at my own pace,
When I slip through stars in empty space,
To breath again Universal Mind,
To live once more in Universal Peace,
To swim for long fathoms the Universal Sea.

So make me a silence to surround
The living peace of burial mound,
Remember Life, Remember Life,
This one thing you can still do for me...
Remember *Life!*

Ten Times The Time

Take ten times the time of living,
Go multiply this act by ten,
Subtract one while standing at the cottage door
And greet yourself arriving home again,
Greet yourself arriving home again,
The pathway trod as simple as a stone sits
Unmoved upon the speeding Earth;
A million raindrops pattering the roof
Smooth the tiles down to their dark
Centre beaches and cave
In to the mountains of the sea
There to rest,
To fly off in unthinking wind
Whirled to the thirsting beat of the sun,
To juggle their worlds into clouds
Wrapping solidity by virtue of vapour,
The grace of gasses.

Hello and time again,
The speckled round,
The upward curve of your face
Greeting the morning clock the sky,
Hello and time again,
The tenfold and hallowed round;
Sighing mornings of All Sounds and Time Again.

The River Sacred And A Tree

Think you upon a river,
Muse upon a tree,
Think upon the future,
On all that may ever be.

Sacred the earth, and so hill,
Sacred the river flowing beneath,
Sacred the sky which clouds try to fill,
Sacred the tree, and so leaf.

Sacred the ocean, mantle of Life,
Sacred grass, stone and air,
Sacred the blood, the shield and knife,
Sacred the cell and the breadth of a hair.

Sacred the word in lilt and in tone,
Sacred the thought of mercurial mind,
Sacred the eye, the ear and the bone,
Sacred the dust ashes we all leave behind.

Think upon a river.
Think upon a tree.
See the colourless waters clothe themselves
To be with colours.
See these waters bend playing
Light, bend themselves and shape the land.

Muse upon an ocean,
On great seas' depth,
Their weight of water
Weighing nothing
Within your hand.

Think upon the one
Lead metal of the World
Weighing nothing, turning
Upon Itself in space,
Slow, silent, sacred Earth where we work and play
Each and all moment sacred,
Where we live and turn with it, sacred.

Sacred the stars, and so space,
Sacred the planet, the insect, the beast,
Sacred the action, the step and the pace,
Sacred the kill, the chewing and feast.
Where yesterday we played
We die today.
No-one dies yesterday,
No-one dies tomorrow,
Each shall die today.
So think you upon a river,
Muse upon a tree.

Sacred the growing,
And so generation,
Sacred the wheel,
And so track,
Sacred hearth,
The house and nation,
Sacred the river
Which *never* flows back!

Think you upon a river...
Think you upon a tree....

All Suns Replete

All suns replete the morrow shall not dance
Upon the resting point of former days
Nor boil nor spin the fragrant thought and words
Which melt among the gaps of space above the heads
The smiles of creatures glad to breathe in matter
To swim in breasts of carmine and violet their wings
Their tired limbs revived to the singing winds
Nor shall Chance (that Clown of Fate) fall
Into the seas of happenstance its sharp surprise
No destiny of stars our breath unborn
In silent prayer upon the frozen eye
The lips exultant iced within an enlightenment
Unthought.

69

The Song Of The Shells

Ancient. Ancient. Ancient.
The shells sing of All that has passed.
Ancient. Ancient. Ancient.
So that all good moments may last....

What tells the Clock of All that has gone,
A wave away from the breast of a beach,
Can it be told which hour holds a stone,
What touch has a hand that is just out of reach,
A hand always just out of reach?

What hollow wind blows hot our fate,
Can there be icicles within night's dark fires,
Does mad iron moon burn cold, innate,
How shall we sing our sad soul's choirs,
How sing I of failing ember fires?

A basket of miracles is all we need,
Gold nugget sun spun within the heart,
With plain air wingless for our daily feed,
A waterfall of birds spins my lonely art,
Weave and feather through an only art.

Ancient. Ancient. Ancient.
The shells sing to All that has passed.
Ancient. Ancient. Ancient.
So that all fleshed moments may last....

Say Man if you can where and what is Love?
Pin a butterfly down upon the beach of Time,
Grasp gossamer high farthest star in the right above,
Bring gentle low to this sealed bottle of mine,
Pass it to me while there still lives time,
Be it mine while there still moves time.

My diamond life is hard, the pewter body weak
Falls away with rain a gale in a wreck,

As inner flame sears none then so shall it speak,
A shout, dust of swept words from the Sweeper's deck,
Musty voice from the Sweeper's neck.

Birds drop from clouds their heads a-flame,
Sucked to stone cracks in the narrow day,
Eyes see their throats fall and call out a name,
Her name's widowed by sparrows her neighbours say,
Widowed by wings they say tell.

Ancient. Ancient. Ancient.
The shells sing of All that has passed.
Ancient. Ancient. Ancient.
So that all living moments may last....

With Mind as tall as the sea is long,
Strong is the will and will testify too,
Fine is the line and sheer as a song
Piped by dolphins from the undrowned blue,
Songs sung by fish-tongues in the Untimed True.

It would take a miracle, *yes*, to prise us from the Stone,
At best an adventure begins at everyone's death,
Hear white music in the tomb's one-timed tone,
Stones kiss the ear while bells box beneath,
Bones ring below earth foxing beneath.
Where is my beloved as I hear the cold-table chime,
What destiny awaits the trembling bone?
A single love paid is a love for all time,
The price is *one* lasting moment, one, one, one,
One Eternal Moment yet to be won....

Ancient. Ancient. Ancient.
A shell's song of All that has passed.
Ancient. Ancient. Ancient.
So that all moving moments may last....

Colourless water the colour of praying,
Wet the pumping sound of slapping round cell,

71

The blood veins a fragrance in the slip of saying
While the thought of Her from dear depths plumbs to
swell,
This flask this mask fits my hope true to tell.
She in my slumber holds out sleep-shaped arms,
I plough Her full waves under as I dream far-too-late!
I cannot resist Her spell Her menu of charms,
For I need Her love near and this sole life can't wait;
I walk at the crossroads by the kissing-gate....

So say should you meet Her I stand at the shore,
At the strand place waterline between wet and dry,
Tell Her sure soft that I want Her now evermore,
That the ocean it falls fine frail from mine eye,
That the salt sea it stings in my every sigh,
The malt sea brings wings to my heart from the sky....

Ancient. Ancient. Ancient.
The shells sing of All that has passed.
Ancient. Ancient. Ancient.
So that All our Good Moments will last....

Love, The Singing Tree

Love, the shimmering faun,
Love, the glowing field,
Love, the warm rhythm,
The encircling rhyme,
The crazy metre,
Love, the invisible rope of hearts,
Love, the magnetic pull,
Love, pearl-carved dove,
Love, the tearful joy,
Love, the blue bay in swim,
The iridescent star of dawn,
The laughing highlight,
Is swaying,
Is dancing...
Is *running into sunrise!*

The City Sea

I think of the sea in the city,
The beaute blue waves
Proud bowing,
Tumbling in
The green bay,
The sea air
Trembling
The hair in the wind,
Beneath the foot the dry sand
Zinging
Across wet skin;
Ozone sparks bright,
Draws the inward breath
Through the teeth
Springing
Alert the sea-taunted
Cell haunted,
Alert to the deep height
Seen within a city night...
In the far gaze...
The distant sea.

Ocean thoughts laze in the city,
Deep seen deep waters shimmering
The sun at noon
Sparkling on water the air's breath-
Sprinkled stars of the night,
Marooned on the moon-
Moved rollercoasters under
The sun-baked might
Glimpsed of cliff and heath
Falling
Stone vertical to foam-ocean
Lips where break-waves toast
The sand-fringed finger,
The coastal ghost,
This city sea! How it taunts me!

The distant sea!
Cloud shadow falls
On a day-wet cobweb
In the city; stalls
Within a night vision,
Sea waves darken in memory
To flow and sudden ebb,
To linger on
Only in sea-taunt,
Mind alert to the far haze thought!

Then, in this far night city gaze, sought
No longer the wave-smoothed beach;
Out of reach
The distant sea,
The distant city sea.

I think of the sea
In the city,
The beaute blue waves
Proud bowing,
Tumbling in....

Moth To A Flame, Like

Facet of theatre
The jade-carved stage
Lit by fires
Aflame the unscripted flow
Sculpts scenery in pulse
Of living vein and seeds
Melt to essence of spark
The ember of words
Splintering the falling air
In light flight of fireflies
Lost gliders in heat
Of the Icarus moment
Acted out of the mouth!
Musing chrysalis...
A butterfly explosion!

Drawing

A fine line has been drawn
From probability to a new place
Defined by bells,
A village sea-drenched with flowerbeds
Where hedges glitter with the truth
Of mountains pregnant blue and star-topped
As the smoke of log fires,
Drifting monograms of an initial future,
Etch on honeycombs of cloud
In waxen old-time sunsets
Thin and slow, the sleep of apricots.

Phosphorus light in flushed dark
Crab apple afterglow
Fades in waves as the sea
Dashes a salt lick across
The breathy beach,
Turning pebbles; a million
Insect wing-cases rattle,
Shuffle away into the sideways deep;
Sand glows in the bathing gloom,
Each grain a moon
Toned in tumescence, marvellous in moonlight,
The sharp points of stars ignoring the Earth.

Cool gold oil-skinned sea
Dresses in blackbird's feathers,
Ruffles in water its black roses,
Uncoils its cobras,
Unrolls its carpets,
Unfolds its floor,
And, without the need of cushion or couch,
Settles its great weight down in the bay-bed
For a wingless no-sleep night,
Inky under the frost-lit lid....
Far-off, one time, a twig snaps
And All-Of-A-Sudden! jumps a wave
To a dawn brushed in birdsong....

Nightmare

Mauve movements lurk hidden almost,
Slip crab-sidle lurch from the murk tissue ghost
Corners of unseen flame-struck
Smouldering jump-nerve eyes,
Shadows skulk, overlap to sulk amongst themselves,
Prowling purple pirates
Of some vague land-wrecked hulk,
Lampblack spits cat skulls crossboned in black
Veil mournful limp, slope a dripping howl, torments
Wind-scream choke cowl, midnight eerie cries
A covered dream benighted,
Unmooned lack-star ferments,
Bubbles gross under the closed lid and darkly troubles
The dreaming, frowning brow!

This night, a lead-black tar flag
Unfurled, flaps wild, the skin of a wound
Untended in a storm, and foul skies gush blood to tag
And tremble deep ground rumble-shaking pound
Of ocean, threshes alive a mad masque
In subsonic empathy,
Vibration of tympanic whale skull drumskin,
Bass bone gigantic splits asunder nerve and teeth
In boom-struck caverns dream-deep down
That hold in limestone-salted hands the secret crown
Of deepest sea, underground wash of whirlpool sudden
Crash of searing wave beneath
The dream-scoured, frowning brow!

Ghoul of tooth-black bat-mist cloud grasps at mind,
Swirls a thunder wing across entirety of sky,
Black-bone backbone fingers
Strike out shade night's eye...
Black lacquers, undulates, becomes blacker than blind,
Dim glimmer, flurry of hurling souls in instant hurry,
Scurry of chasing scramble, instincts urge to flush out

The stretched panic, to escape an invisible invisibility
Distinct solely in unformed sharp fear rush,
Gush of heart's liquid vein-jerk racing pelt,
Animal scream sleep-deep raked nail terror rips
The sweated, frown-tight, startle-woken brow!

Take Not The Word I Breathe

Take not the word I breathe
With you through the Timeless Gate,
That portended door,
The crazied edge of shard existence
Which births teetering below push of foot
That feels to tread into cutting chasms,
Unknown territories
Owned by shades,
By shadows, of other, alien lands.

Take not the sword I wield
With you through the faceless stare,
The pictured pore,
The crazy-paving skin of hard existence
Which grows below hush of touch
That feels to tread into Void,
Unknown places owned and dimmed
By shades,
By phantom gloves of alien hands!

Some Silent Time Alone

Muse on other centuries
Some silent time alone...
Think upon All Ages,
Please to turn their beckoning pages,
And, with a reckoning mind
Faceted of moments,
Seek hiding aeons yet to find
The Breath of Life....

This Breath of Life
Yet forms Itself, ferments
Those decades surely poised to come,
Strange days brewed
To unfold
Fresh, a-newed
Beneath stranger suns
So brightly,
So sprightly,
Old....

Muse on days, hand
In hand with the Muse of Hours, and
On weeks now left far, far behind
Seek, from this silvered time of ours,
Sleek dancing down the mind
In unseen silken minuets
To those golden-footed minutes past,
And see the poets leave us as in a breeze,
Their silver-lined and linear ghosts
In most lively legacies!

Think you now upon the many oak-solid poets
Who will *never* breath their last,
Souls wing-spread fixed within
The living resin, or
The walking, talking, fossil of that fleeting mirror
Called sad-illusioned Time;
Hear their wingéd words beat tick-tock

As they flock quicking to our inner clock's
Eternal chime,
Their *very lives* handwritten in
The Collective Heart,
Penned strong to chisel upon
All Humankind's brave
Polished, paved and towering long headstone,
A vasting tomb, true, but a truer, greater tome
Laid clear by pen,
Made dear by open Intuition's art,
To flow in open rivers,
To grow impassioned from their silent giver's fingers,
To sow and seed in sweeping linear grace
Their curve and loops of lines
With the lovely, perfect, complete poise
Of countless gleaming generations,
The prose of gene limbed elegant,
The softing eyes and smooth gyrations
Of poems seen within a Timeless face,
Words that fall as water falls
To descend with unceasing race,
Or as robes drape a lasting body
Simply dressed,
Blessed of a cloth cut of rhythm,
Sewn of rhyme,
Shaped of verse and spun of time
Made firm and tailored fine
By the living blood of finning verse and fun
In an everlasting story's hearty pun...
But if their lines should some black day
(...O how unthinkable!...)
Spend to die and in mould descend
To rot and go, become forever sinkable,
Without again one reading eye for friend,
Then, in no doubt, I would say
(As I meditate on how Shelley might
Have talked with stones at night
Or sung sweet to stars, called to lightning
Or flung his young arms wide to greet the sun),

The Poem,
For real, could *never* have been *ours*,
Could *never* have breathed under moon or sun,
It could *never* have even been begun
To become as if a lovers' kiss
Left imprinted upon the heart
Of some cheeky Miss,
Or better (so to firmer grasp the feeling of the age)
Placed by truly loving lips upon the page
Of a tear-streaked, sole and cherished,
Sadly sage
Last love-letter,
Written one to Darling One
Some silent time, alone....

The Devil's Song

Unless you spend your Time
To strike me down in height of Summer fields...
The less the Day shall rest and all the Night
Be *mine* to dance and suck within your Breath
My towered life of dark suns suspend about my breasts
Your Life tucked within mine sweated gland
Shall never know that carriage low
Nor sight nor sense of *Good*
Will flow in sparkled demon dawns
Through Innocent's wood and Heart once your own
Sole soul now *mine* to burn..... as...
Dross fuel that sharpens horn to thrust
That, nimble, brings to hobbled tread
In obscene dance, skin of skirts above the head,
Your malformed soul exposed that I twist
Would call its gargled cry of gargoyles
To the darkening sky and fetid wind insist,
Loathe to smell your last death breath I own
That I offer to the Clock tick tock
Unless you spend your Time to strike me down
In height of Summer fields my Clown! *Hah!*

Dawn Horus Poem

Slow to rise, the circled sun
Fans light up
To feed gold upon
The treacled Horus-cup
Of every ocean's weight
Upon the land,
Lightfoot cast with Horus-hand,
Over clean-cut straight
And melting sea's continual
Mould of molten metal,
Simmering, glows onto
Liquid-mirage horizon!

There is but one horizon far-
Rings the globe, one star-
Measured mean eye-line,
And it moves,
This paced skyline,
And it proves
The roundness of the sky
In the soundness of the eye!

Slow to rise, the circling sun,
Pans light down and
Filters fluttering first-rays' golden,
Horus-hovering, gleams upon the ground
Of every mountain's weight
Upon the land,
Lightfoot cast with Horus hand
Over rain-cleaned slate
And hot dried, heat-fried,
Shimmering deserts' continual
Mould of molten, reddened metal,
Simmering, blows onto
Liquid mirage horizon!

This one horizon far-
Creams the World, one star

81

Twilight-seen skyline...
And it moves,
This spaced eye-line,
And improves
The soundness of the eye
In the roundness of the sky!

The Thread We Run

The thread we run
Is thin as sun
Light.

O my Angel! take to flight...
You *alone* have wings!
It is enough to rise
Above all things
To soar in clear and unobstructed skies!

There are footprints on the river,
I hear passed footsteps in the sand,
Though it is only wind-rush power
Tugs now strong my empty hand....

Are you gone forever, pray,
Where are you now in *absentia?*
Are we to hold phantom hands
Or ride in Freedom on our Way?
Where your ghost my airsome one?
O *you* I'll not forget!

The thread we run
Is thin as sun
Light.

O my Angel, take to flight!
You alone have *wings....*

82

Dusky

Dusky, She is the moon
Behind storm cloud,
Appearing to me
From raw depths of dreams,
Utter blackness sudden brightening
In one loud hissing strike
Of lightning
That creams the swirl dark,
A dank ozone, musky
Animal odour, salt keen and tight,
Invisible bonds pulled open
By a scythe-moon night.

Dusky, She descends
From Her spark-lit fires,
Lives and advances slow, sure
Serene and azure
Yet with the power of oceans
Or full-sailed juggernauts ridden
Over vast seas,
Waves of unbidden
Visions, dreams
Driven, riven
Through opium-washed veins, seams
Of gold-wrought vermilion, scenes
Woven by night
Dream indigo hands.

Dusky, There She stands
The Never-Old,
Born of Ancient Lands,
Hills echo drums of thunder,
Peals of bells unfold
Around, over and under,
Through air that abounds
In pounding energy,
A pulse that tells
Of secret stores

83

Of existence; She holds
Out Her hand, a pearl
Upon lined palm to gladden
Hearts; makes my life dance
Lest it should sadden
On that strange, calm cadence,
The ethereal stark-souled shore!

Dusky, She awakes All Desire,
And I desire life more
When, with soft fingers' silver tips
She touches dainty light my mouth,
Makes smiles
Appear on Her lips
And mine; a sliver of tear
Slithers south,
Streams down a joy
Clothed in the gown
Of our long hours;
She gives me presents of dreams
Wrapped in toy
Maps of all the stars
Which She found
Quite by chance
(or so it seems),
Where look meets glance,
A riddle,
A tremble-space
Of uncountable time
In the blue very middle
Of our gaze line.

Dusky, *near!* She has drawn near,
A turban wrapped of live snake
Swathes her dark
Obsidian-masked head,
And I, startled *awake!*
Here, in my nighttime bed,
Yawning dreams vanish in

Dimmed flakes of banished
Snake-scale skin;
They shudder and fall
Into new light
Beam of sunrise
Marble-shine hall,
Clear void of black flight
Fingers of falling rivers
Of nightjar jitters,
Of Dusky soft-calling
Nights!

Darkness

Darkness is my friend
Slips a hand in mine
Covers the skin close
Joins with the dark beneath
As we stroll along
As I tread out into her
Invisible folds
Caress the cheeks the lips
Play soft with the hair
Smooth the airy palm from neck to flank
More of sense than sight
More of touch than scent
More of taste than sound
Slight dent of lip the black teeth
Grin unseen
Wraps the widened eye
Without effort
Without movement
Without blindness
Without a care
In grace of shadows...
I *see* Her!

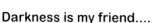

Darkness is my friend....

After A Dry, Hot Spell

Small round mirrors flash the smoke air,
Dash to crash and dare, falling
As rain, fall dropping down, there and there and there...
And *here* to steam-heat dance,
Fast to globe, to mimic Earth-shape, and glance
Their tears of every epoch's years askance,
As they full jump
Away from ground's vertical pull, and lump
Pop and leap to quicksilver bump
Along sun-fried late day's pavements, skid to
Stop and splash, and in a moment hid, to
Rush and die as gush fades the dusk upon
Musk Summer foot-kissed and cooling stone
To shine away wry-washed scenes
Through emptied streets that in warbling streams
Lace worm-wriggle neon city beams in puddled water!

The high-colour blush
Light of sudden waters' rush
Hones the stone, gentle flushes drought dust,
Whisks brisk down sparkling gutters
Full-pooled,
Whirlpooled water-gift
Stutters through a concrete night
That tight pulls and holds hard
The shard land,
Covers velvet and clings the glassy strand,
While the shivering towers
Surrender to the grassy grand
Freshness of the blackening pearl
Night-imp, their neat and many-gardened bowers....
Night descends to blanket a darkening swirl
With late evening's moon-hid and hiding powers!

I furl the curtains closed
Upon the poised and posed,
Deep rich-eyed and bright city night
With a speckled, moist and street-lit hand....

Her One Name

Whosoever has seen within
A clinging night-mist
The silver bones of a tree, Winter-bare,
Come looming up stark sudden
As if from nowhere,
Unbidden, spectral,
The eerie fanning rays of a hidden light
Full-beamed behind it, can (I'm sure) imagine
How Her head and unkempt hair
Ghostly branched awry upon it
Appears to my inner sight as She slowly turns
To me in deepest dreams,
Where, within some imploring time
She calls in vasting echo,
Her eyes aglow and mouth
Wide in fearsome yawn,
Howls mournful in goosefleshed cry
Her One Name...!...
Always forgotten upon awakening!

Rabbit Tundra

Rabbit tundra
Layered earth terrine
In running animal fold
Of furred field
Muscled tense over the rock
Mounted hills of bone white
Stone the leaping vision wide
Before the burrowing push
Beneath the rushing hawk
The damp of safe soil sniffed
To cradle the twitching nerve
Alive the dead earth verve...
Alive and living yet....

87

Badlands

Waterless...
A parch-souled Summer,
Waterless out of hell hot hob swell,
Out of the bell
Throat a dry rasp,
Waterless as shed snakeskin
In unslaked sum of gasp,
Waterless, grim of melt,
Drip of burning metal smelt,
Waterless, tinder trees lisp,
Bushes burn bone crisp
And waterless,
The flake-skin soul-spark falls
To dust, waterless,
Slate and roofs and backs split asunder,
Waterless under
Sun-heat oven crust waterless,
Sky-dry cataract kilns the crumbling earth,
Eyes waterless,
Life shed root shrivels to skeletal girth,
Waterless within the grinning worm, clay smokes,
Demons laugh in crackled cackles, raw jokes
Of all waterless in their paper-charring pits and chokes,
Fire-licks wilt the crack of unanchored seed,
Shrivels to parchment rustle the sap stem and slows all
speed,
It splits and fades the bending head of flower,
Bleaches rock,
Unholy blood bursts the swollen tongue of arching lock,
Clouds burn, tip sharp to rip the slipping reservoir dry,
Rifts the crack of stone, puckers the pout of waterless
thigh,
Heads nowhere and hardens the cave of nerve, the
shrivelled eye,
Shredded water rushes up the unseen hairs of airless
deep,
Waterless cell sews its skin tight, life to rein in and keep.

Salt sucks in the brittle bone sand,
Gathers baked white on thin yellow,
Rock splits and pits to sand,
Waterless shrink and mellow
Sand grains rattle,
Fall and flow through the unquenched vein,
Through hollow tube of bone,
Ravishes terrain waterless, siphons the dried,
Sharpened hone of flint-sparked grass
Dry through the wasted, waiting time of waisted
hourglass,
Through rainless deserts' killing grasp,
Waterless out of the bell throat a powder-rasp,
Unslaked waterless fire ash Summer gasp
Baked waterless out of run-dry fountainhead,
Dead out of hell-hot hob-tongued swell,
Waterless...
And the starless night is almost white, waterless
Riven riverbed of split-souled Summer day waterless,
All water *gone*, spent and sped, fled to the poles...
Waterless....

Joker

Man you are just some kind of other ape
Stirring the ocean with gaping grin,
Grimace of foolishness over your chin,
Hoping wild for jumping fish to flash
Ornamental in your matted hair,
Flying thoughts effortlessly driven
Over some sad edge....

Dribble and paddle sorry ape doodler
Drying the ocean with your aimless finger,
Fiddling the shoaled strings rippling,
Hoping mild for flying fish to dash
Excited into your itching sad palms,
Jumping thoughts simply ridden
Over some mad edge....

Dragon Fight

The footstep knows no place
Nor finds a tread
Timid, timid time stopped...

Upon the air-filled brink
Has such a breath as would burn
All as soon as lit
The reptile coil unleashed
Sudden deadly to the vein
Fluid, fluid time begun
Upon the air-filled brink
Has such a pace as would transfix
All as soon as bit,
The subtle foil unsheathed
Sudden deadly to the scale
Limpid, limpid time is cut
Upon the air-filled brink
Has such a look as would hypnotise
All as soon as hit
The flame of life released
Sudden deadly to the worm
Morbid, morbid time in rot
The footstep finds no pace
Nor knows a time uncropped
Upon the air-filled brink
Has such a depth as would drop
All as soon as fled to myth
The obscure act enshrined
Sudden deadly to the heart, the mind...
The footstep knows no place!

I Dance The Dusts

I dance the dusts, the emerald dusts
That fly in green fires kicked
Up from the dirt-track path in sparkle
Where meadows undulate their star fields to grace
In sapphire magnetic the wide-boughed trees
Where whorled galaxies slow spin
Between wide-spread branches
Weighted in jewels,
Where planets orbit swift
Fireflies bright as eyes
Genius of intelligent suns in crystal focus
In solitary muse on time in space
To mushroom from out the spangled grasses
Unexpected in surprise of gleams,
A scintillate carousel delight
Universal diamond breath which draws me on....

I am a comet paving a path
To open in gold the encrusted casket
As I rush towards treasures...
A *gem* of dawns!

The Spell Trees

Old sorcerers wave windy, jump crazy-limbed,
Leap and gesture at the edge
Of fields; trounce and dance
Wild in the wind, wild in the wood,
A spell of trees....
Storm leaf-lost wizards in a bounce of gale
Dart sharp-twig fingers from air-spread hands,
Cast come-alive spells to frost-hard and hiding ground,
Swirl-branch arms whip, twist-twirl, enchant again
In the slash-cut cruel and sleet-riddled rain,
Wood in the wind,
Wood in the wild,
Wild in the witchy wood,
A spell of trees....

Rest Easy Little Soul

Rest easy, little soul, rest easy,
All things that turn about themselves are simple,
Stars, the humble river and sheltering tree,
Wood grain and placid bird, sun and weaving mineral,
Laugh and song and cheeky dimple,
True are all, plain as they can be,
So gaze on this incessant world consistent,
In wordless joy and wonder, and you shall see
A singular beauty, inherent.

Rest easy, little soul, rest easy,
All things that turn about themselves are simple,
And all things must turn around, eventually...
Rest easy, little soul, rest easy,
Lay your anxious head here, awhile, with me.

The Waves Don't Part

The waves don't part along the shore,
Crest-line curls a certain course,
Curves to break in whited walls a roar
Heard in forest winds or
From invisible source of woven growth.

The waves won't part along the shore,
Beach-break binds a bowed intent,
Bends to curve the white sand maw
In rippled lips of torrent
Tumble to form anew the flesh
Of bone-rib lands.

The waves don't part along the shore,
The stars watch sure their flecked tread
Across salted skies of ebony raw
That hold the sleepless dead
Within their airsome arms,
Their solid breath.

December Storm

Clouds let fall a sea,
Leafless countryside weeps a flood
Under the deluge of dark
Waters downpouring incessantly....

Wrapped in night, plough-parked
Earth clods break to flow as thin mud
And stones protrude wet from this blood,
Bones exposed in an unseen, upturned face.

Seething rivulets turn into streams that run to rivers,
Grow quickly wide and quick to race
Over fields to wash the land in ways diverse
With fearsome might of elemental force.

This December storm can be heard bell-clear,
Though little presents itself to sight,
I wonder where wet birds might find shelter
As I walk home late within a wet and weary night.

Hours later and most clouds have fled,
The land surprisingly silent as I gaze about
To see that upon each plant- and twig-head
Sparks a dew-star, as bright moon orbs out.

Bush, tree and grass, all silent on their soaking ground,
Shine with a myriad constellations as if in greeting
To the stars above in their fixed and orbiting round;
I wonder, do their cells recall some ancient tryst,
Some treasured star-souled last kiss of affinity
Remembered now at this, their latest fleet-foot meet
Across the deep gulf of Infinity?

A Dancer In Dreams

A dancer in dreams,
She tumbles within the swathes
Of her femininity;
Its volumes billow
About her as she bathes
Inside.

The whispers to her pillow
Are her inmost secrets,
Shared solely with linen.

You Should Not Gaze On Me

You should not gaze on me so direct,
Your face, as the fast full-moon would,
Could wane to fall waxen, shipwrecked
Below the Greater Sea to soon
Be *gone...!*

(The gaze of certain women
 Has such a look,
 One
 Sole
 Stare
 Can hypnotise, read you like a book and then
 Enthral to the exclusion
 Of all else, until anything *other*
 Becomes Illusion; O yes! I can tell you this, my brother!
 I say... Eyes! *Be Gone...!)*

So my *only,*
My *one* lovely,
Do not rest your eyes on me,
Your face full-turned,
Lest we both melt into that Greater Sea:
A lively living would be spurned
And our encircled heart and your ringing beauty
By our own hand suddenly
Be *gone...!*

94

The Spirit-stone

So thin, the thinnest thin,
A molecular wafer, waved
And glassy smooth, fluid mirror,
A light-flare starred water-skin
That covers all, moves
From welling source of rising spring
To sea and river delta,
To cling, to ring and wrap,
To cover sheer sheen gleam
Over vast seas undulating flap
Form, a mantle-spirit born
Of water, of air, modulating
A curved soft-swell change
As of wind-tossed hair or grasses' billow
Under meadow willow
Fronds that weave and wave
Their leaf-paved pillow,
While branches of midday trees
Reach up into opal scrying skies
Flown only by lone eagles
That, flying, crying spy
Their own spread-wing
Reflection echo-image
With sharp and beaded eye.

Then over whispered waters,
Flowing chuckle deep,
Sped by Earth's hard spirit,
A flying stone appears; it
Rucks and tucks with yawing leap,
Plummets fast across the polished deep,
Does fair wind and blow,
Speed and go...
A rounded pebble disk
Skim-thrown through toned and tight-tensioned air...
Spun as quick as a risk
Taken with tic-tac flip flash of wrist

Is sped slick-fast as a myriad days
Disappear into red set suns,
Days spent by this planet's race,
As our spinning stone land-run
Sends a spawning pace
About the sun...
With owlish silence
Our black and shiny Spirit-stone
Whorls a paralleled path,
To sudden flat-sting sharp upon thin divide reflex dance
Of shimmer-mirror skin;
This Stone rises and levels in,
Almost hovering to alight...
Again smack-hits and hops and dips
On, through mirror-images of black throat nights,
And skims beneath starless days
In the shot-silk haze
Of a myriad boiling suns....

It is a bird this flying Stone,
A slicing, jiving, levelled rock skim-bouncing,
Trouncing air and clear sheer skin...
Flees the whip-wrist bone
From flesh twist-wrist sling
To fly over the lean surface thread-thin layer,
A film of breath, a spirit-prayer...
It spins to travel,
To explore
A track that, unravelled,
Moves more and more
Forwards and up
As it sings towards the shaped-flesh cup
Of the waiting, stilled,
Skilled hand shaped
By the Catcher who, with eager hands, stands
Upon the banked and guiding lands
Of the further shore.

When the Stone reaches
There is a turnabout,

As in taken tumble-turn
Catcher becomes Thrower,
And with power
Turns about
And quick-flick throws back....

Once more the roundel skims,
Keens and creams along
As ripples
Spread hoop-circle nipples
Where it strong
Hits soft and licks
Thin top of fathom's depth-fount
(Where fine-lead water ferns unfurl),
Mounts and twists about, upon
Thin facet water cover...
It spins and whorls headlong
Along, our Spirit-stone...
It lively hops and belly-flops, looms over
Shine shrine surface
Of a million moons or more,
Tips and tilts above,
Taps and slaps and kisses a course
Which planes and angles flat
As flying fishes
That love, fin to fin
With salty seaweed wishes,
And our Spirit, our Stone, swishes
To the far-won shore.

Lesser flat stones, flat,
All momentum soon spent,
Sink below to glide beneath,
Slant-eye down silk waters
To the flood graves of minnows,
Slant-slip-slide fall, zigzag and snake,
Fade wetly in those darkening pits
Of oceans, of seas, of lakes,
Of rivers, that winding crawl
And sprawl to meet white waves...

While our turning, twirling Stone wheels,
Its spirit clipping through ink-blackened
Nights unlit, keels
And flits through clear days brave,
To stride and step-stone tag
Bridge-span arcs of dashing,
Tide-splashing rings, where dance-light
Sirens sing sun-bright jiggling, juggling songs.

Our skipping touchstone
Winnows, stuttered swift and sure
Over atom mirror, on mercurial water skin's
Blue shimmering and green haze-heat; fleet
As if pulled by strings,
Our Spirit-stone with invisible wings
And claws, with unseen feet,
Hones on to balm-palmed lands,
Where It, from subtle-sensed hands,
Homes in to spring swimming
Upon other distant shores full-brimming!

I Sing Operatic To The Stars

I sing operatic to the stars
This poem ever on to lead to light,
I dream and sport decisions strong, dip dreams' oars
To move evergreen between rivers of trees
Through a crisp and hiding Winter night.

My single lamplight throws one dark shadow
And I journey with a blink and wide-eyed stare
As, bending unseen to their wood wend
In the hard and covering earth below,
Loops the slender searching ways of root.

And Winter chill is the crystal, frosting air
In cloak of ice and freezing, silent-falling soot
Beneath clear cloudless pearl-domed skies,
Where, from the black invisible, sparkled eyes,
All-seeing, seem to turn and look on me...
Worlds without End...!

The Butterfly

My heart, the butterfly,
Filled in petals graced of dew
Wings away on wings
Yet does not leave the breast
A sweet hunger unfulfilled
Essence of nectar sipped gentle
The butterfly is of itself refreshed
Is of itself renewed!
Constant now
My heart, the butterfly....

Undisputed Islands

Undisputed islands nest within the sea;
Their aura of wetness drops to horizon's blur,
Dissolves tremble-finger shores
Where sleek cascades of sand grains waterfall,
Undermine
The arms of palm trees,
Expose roots bare to tropical sun and storm;
Grasses bristle,
Cling to line inner island round of shelter
Where silence broods mute egg and seed
Harboured within nest shadow gloom,
A twilight fine-balanced point
Beneath eggshell clouds
Under eyebrow moons
Throughout the beaking crack of dawn's light
Breached by brightnesses,
The salt-blown tumble
Skies moist in streaming air,
Warm to endless swell of heated ocean
Beaches.
The hiding scattered dust of islands
Are coral stepstones bare
Where Dream's tiptoe reaches out
In stretch of light-touch seek.

And, And, And, And, And....

The cloaks of ages grace as dew,
Patina this enduring form,
Wrap their elegant libation,
Their salt myopic,
Their clouds of glycerine balm
To the yet living skin
Spectre of breath prescience,
The soft strength of ancient waters
Smoothing out the wrinkles
Between moments
Cased in experience.
Tough sight, sense
The coming years!

April Devon Sunrise

Slow to rise the circled sun in power of lemon.
Morning streams in silver warm-touch,
Young light splinters through slumbered mists
In a shower of opal, sleep-late dreams.

Silent, dawn feathers a wing-shake,
Twig-foot birds testing New Light's breath-light sight
In wonder of warming, nestled bowers.

Tuning day poises lazy, hazily wanders,
Uncoils its slow-worm snaking spring
Through sun-beamed, oak-beam towers
Brimming birdsong!

Cloaked vales wake bared, silk veil vapours vanished,
Supped soft up to fire-thirst throat of sun
In fading flowers of crystal cloud.

Slow to rise, the circled sun climbs the blue
In power of lemon!

The Moor Wind

The moor wind is
Thrumming,
Drumming,
Running spike-foot 'cross the open moor;
It drums the Earth,
Pumps a mocking mirthed hiss,
Chill smoothes in stone-face shock
Moor's sun-blanched bones,
Pits weathered rock,
Slashes a sleeting curse horizontal,
Scours, pours hysterical,
Hones, grinds
Each ancient lintel
And levels the land,
Sands every rock-face it finds
With the persistent chisel-hand
Of Time....

The wilding wind is
Thrumming,
Drumming,
Watch it climb the silvered ladder of the sky....
Eye-storming gale is strumming
Over chilled
And cowered moor,
Drags the Earth down
Screaming
Louder even than the air-filled,
Vacant bellies of this planet's poor....
Watch it crown
The eye, climb the loose and breaking sky....

The wilder wind is
Brimming,
Skimming
Across the mild-fleshed moor...
It sprints in gaseous bliss,
Drums and runs the good Earth

And tears its tangled hair...
Watch it rip the streamered sky
And pluck the heart from its living eye....
It thrums loud,
This girthing mask
Of birthing Earth; watch
It comb the freezing cloud
And, floating high, catch
And flask
The whistling, fleeing sky!

A Question Of Civilisation

That expression of the machine upon your face,
From where does it spring or spring not,
Flitting across those ancient-bred features
As does the shadow of a moth against the fire
That feeds the furnace of automatic impulse
Until that flame melts of its own mechanical heat,
To gutter and goat in extinction of wings?

That expression on your face
Of the pressed metal sheeting which smiles
Against those tombstone teeth,
Does it grow there in all natural locomotion,
Restrained ecstasy of the civilised cell,
Or does it, clouds wafting across
The craters of the moon,
Have no real substance,
Ectoplasm melt on the glass slide?

That machine in grin upon your face,
That cog of feigned delight,
That liquid mercury smear at run above your solid chin,
Where is its sulphuric source of ored stone fount,
Its roots hidden dark down deluded ages,
Twist and chancre of the burned nerve,
The continual drift to cliffs of Oblivion, over and over?

Out Of The High Night Reaches

Out
Of the high night reaches
The more-tired-than-sleep,
More-dead-than-ash powdered phoenix zero
Flew my thought, my bird, my love steep
Sheltered in constant wish for peace and placebo,
A moon-loved word in a head full of beaches,
Warm and weather,
Curl and feather,
Full-lipped wonder of woman and the sea,
One birth-clipped thought clipping man-flesh to be
A spark-charged magnificence at bay to go
Luminous, a halo within a void black day limbo,
To spin and guess, to crimp the half-glimpsed way
Out.

In
To the flesh made wisdom,
To the towering wave in the lens night,
To the salt-cell-at-cipher all-in-a-weather foam,
Lather the back-to-back coast in glories of starlight
To fly aloft and love in an equal height the woman
Of the rags of plenty,
The opened cloud of fin and feather or man barren
Of the nimbus surrounding, the placid call for sons,
A knotted peace or not, mildew and fever,
Feverfew and daisy between the darkness,
Held by magnetism, the moon, the seasons,
A lit filament forever forks to undress
That woman of means; my one, my lover, take my
caress
In.

Across
The quick waters of a glance,
Forever ever in the sole stream,
Flow and fishes in this sea cry liberty
At seaweed undoing and dance,

103

At the bowed trance wave licking sand in a dream,
At the lovely windy woman her sails a sea
And rucking in the breezes of my thought,
Wave and womb the far satellites wooing,
Tip tall and climb after
The world of wonders in a gale of water,
The ocean within, a teared bottle floating
Deep as an inside feeling as long as a draught
Of living galaxies and a wish, a meteor zing
Across.

Down
Down
Down the base
Blind spot sailing through
The ether; a flame on a halo holy,
Wicked water burning the cruel glue
Of bound circumstance and seal, part or wholly
True on the weather-climbed hill, the taste
Of thunder in the teeth, rock and rain rattling after
Identity like a witch doctor at prayer,
The tongue the pierced soothsayer,
The bone-pointed slayer,
And the colour of water, falls, sighs in my thought,
A comet in a storm of dripping scales, scythes, climbs
Down.

Under
The far-flung reaches, forward for union,
The lowest point strokes the fur of settling
Dust of rock and time wishes, hurls a thought
To the air speeding towards an unknown
Receiver tuned to miracles within the One Void,
Spinning like a bride in a bed of drills,
Hunting for the aerial which spikes the crown
To receive a homing charge sparked to android
Comprehension of metal spires and mandrills,
The beat heart within adverb suspended,
Copper roof of a valve in the bivalve sea

Flicks into life the veined nerve, fled below
To return as wife by the shade in the shadow
Under.

Through
It all again and again the sorrowed veil,
And black is the whole dug by night
In the cool, fine beaches of Oblivion's cave,
Melt in the dew-cast rule, the wheel of all tunes,
Covert the net-covered creature with your sight
As shadows peel from the Throne of Light
To grind their rind of parts and disappear in the dunes
Of her face, revealed as pirates or sailors too brave
Until the land has risen as tall as a planet,
Wide as shoulders in the bouldering silence,
With influence strong as the moon raves
And the plants move living, slow as a growing,
Moon-fall timed to perfection,
The moving minutes set and move
Through.

In
To the flesh the glowing wonders,
Bright as freshness as the glowing ponders, black
Into space, travelling as tall as a tower,
As thin as a whisper,
My thought in the still lover, the country stile waits
The invisible tread of a naked walker,
Around the corner of trees bushes a rainbow,
Curves over under the stars in dawn's dim back
And turns to reveal cities in the leaves darker
Than unconscious black,
Shined by the weather into bells, and the *ting*
Of a tinkling stream in the blood of the day,
A calling reverberates down the years in Time's wallow,
The reeds calling the sway bittern hollow, calls the day
In.

Last
Of my lover, the Queen of Beggars, the wise

105

Lover under the eyelid, the Lovely Lady of Ladles
Ladles my thought into wishes which yearn for her only,
My lover my hull, my vibrant vixen of flowing,
Her boat made of glass, of weed, of paddles, solely
Turns in the twilight a veil in the air, a twig
On the tide in my dreams, a halo glowing
Around each of its cells, nimbus and nodule,
Lotus and raiment, cause and trumpet of libido,
Do go to the holy-roly lover my keel lonely
And built in the builded air as a curve, as a fig,
A succulent fruit of the Anima, the lover of Unrule,
The adversary of the Fool,
The Embracer, the one who writes
Last.

Out of the high night reaches
Her hand....

Only The Tip

Only the tip is seen, and that dimly...
Unexpected beginnings itch hesitant below,
Unannounced atoms displayed unseen
In molecular shade formation of life spiral
Thrall within, deep within the chained deep,
Shadow weeping, manacle a weighted shuffle
That, in desperate effort, kicks to bulk and rise
Thoughtless in arched instinct, and blow
Along low-level bedrock of enigmatic sleep
In oblivion of diving blind the shut eyes,
Churn spinning within their sinister, luckless muffle,
Swim and shudder down the murky hidden,
To again upsurge to gain
And vault the closed lid,
One day to breach and fly free...
A dance of peace in clear air's wide scope,
A dance of hope in happy open simplicity.

Sip The Optic

You suck me in through your eyes,
So sup the optic,
Sip the nerve-stemmed glass,
Drink full-lidded in
These full-lipped words
Through cornea crystal,
Eye-test their bouquet,
Their textured maturity,
Savour with tear duct tongue the taste,
Weigh the fluid measure
As viscous tears run within the clear vessel,
Sip the optic dry,
Or sweet, on this white- or red-
Lettered day to assure
The rosé line,
The full-bodied paragraph...
Study how from the neck they bubble,
Phrase poured from print decanter,
And pass sentence
On their giddy source;
Toast the deep cellar
Where adverbs rack with nouns,
Jostle juicy pronouns and onomatopoeia,
While adjectives, grown on the north side
Of the verb-yard,
Join a wordy little wine,
Idioms and metaphors in dusty profusion,
Bottled symbols, bottoms up,
Corked cheers from the prologue cup;
Dated labels suck the optic,
And if you can, still, half-cut read
All the small print,
Move the square-cut cheese aside
(I give you a toast, "Here's mud in your eye!")
So you may eat, or drink, my words....

Driftwood

Pith throb-root snakes to suck clay pap,
Drinks liquid up from marry of soil and stone matrix,
Life-pulse resin in rondo of rebus root-tap
Malmseys skyward through grain
Of mizzen tall vein sky stiff,
Pumping sap yeasts to splay-head medulla hood
To roundel orbit-cell in spin of leaf-swum lakes,
Spreads fronds' flotilla an oak beam armada sail-fixed
Good of supple wood,
Of harboured spinneys in sweep of silent copsing glide,
Float of foliage mainsails wave over glades
The soft-sipped sun to leaf-tip take
In light-shock sway and cradle rocking rustle,
Bustle and shuffle in air-waved draught of air-food,
Flock of green swarms live above earth-marl hide,
Forest tumbles bottle green
To fall and ride of coast and sea,
Waves wake to call the cool
Chlorophyll-coloured leaf-veined breeze,
Ocean wags white-tail breaks to dog
The sandy flag of land,
Whisper of wet-limbed salt greets the grit
Of smoothed sand-seed,
The main-bobbed bay bristles
Blue-green bubbles in silken moiré gland,
Coats salt frost in saline crisp,
Ices firm stem and lizard leaf,
Tree skin fibre-stepping
Trunk- and bark-taste breath to tease,
Whilst, deep underground,
Under overhang, deep-sound waters wait
Each tree's slip and fall in full-bellied belief
Of eventual twig and sprig rotation slow glide and slide
Of each bole and bark-beamed joist,
As root branchings cling to simple wear of cliff
And persistent gnawing gouge of supporting ground

Scooped beneath by inching action
Of ocean's feline stroke
As snake-root grips in, digs in
Clawing action down petrified decades
Their ancestral anchors to firmly found;
But sea licks sure, paring under
To plane away spoked roots' grip
And shave bare the age-striated chin of solid stone
Until tree bole cracks to plunge and timber
Below to wet-shored sandbar hunger and thirst,
Falls rushing, strikes, plank and pip
Burst asunder at laughing ocean lip,
Tongued tide tugs at wood,
Sucks leafy stem into mollusc mouth
And soon sea-worms coil and chew
On fat within wood bone,
Spiralled tunnels open through woody sea-smell tissue
While wave-felled timbers are tossed to spin and spume
In moon-pulled waters' vast issue,
Pitch and yaw within the jaw
Of ocean's white and crested lap
Far from coasts clothed in furl of sipping leaf or dip
Of rooting mingle and hoist
Of arching, branching arms which lift lowly
Earth to bless in greening kiss the blue-blown sky,
Cursed to wander distanced from the green-tint shelter
Of dawn-chorused one-time home
To birds and scampered scurry
Of woodland creatures' run and hurry,
Doomed to roam and bob and waterlog-beam
The steaming seas for seeming centuries
In flat-glass calm and storm-slashed helter-skelter,
In curve of careering starlit course adrift.
Bathed and bleached
By constant sun in the salt-bone smile
Of whaling, sharking tides, fathom-floundering
Mile after mile
To one day when, sudden, the natural craft

$\Longrightarrow$

From sea is sprung
And its long lost raft is jettisoned, flung
Foaming from the cave of spume-waved core
To land, a single, rounded driftwood spar
Cast up on sand by mould of night-sea's animal paw,
Beached and phosphorus-pored in skin of burning stars
To bask and moon upon some sea-songed alien shore,
A lone and lonely testament to oceans' might,
Forevermore.

I Don't Know

I don't know what was seen
Half in, half out, of sleep,
That stirred the brow,
That formed the thought,
That opens sight to World.

I don't know what was thought
Half in, half out, of sleep,
That restored sound,
That formed the world
That reveals light to Mind.

I don't know what was heard
Half in, half out, of sleep,
That sensed itself,
That moved the lid
That plays the note of Life.

I don't know what was felt
Half in, half out, of sleep,
That caught the touch,
That drew the form
That lives the Dance of Life.

The Sibyl Of Jewels

Over the high wind race
Sharp stars trace
Steady above,
Space for years
Upon untold years
Silent as snowfall
Caught within a valley deeper
Than dark dip of Winter solstice.

They gleam and spark
As highlights upon unseen eyes
With lids sky-dark
Might, with a myriad reflections,
Blink and peep
To the Unattainable
In thrall
Of some far destination,
So shine they stellar
To the cellar of low
Proud hills below
That speak soft and sing tall
To the gem-crests of the Impossible
In upward urge, and pitch their peaks
With desire to attain a glimpse of the invisible
Star-clothed Sibyl of Jewels!

Over the high wind pace
Sharp points lace
Steady above,
Adorn the sibylline breasts of this void queen
With glorious fire
Of gorgeous gems,
Winged in sapphire,
Flown in white and flecked in green,
Rayed and arrayed to the clustered hems

Of a vast cloth galaxy-rich
In deeping colours, in liquid stone glow,
A gleamed and black-gloved treasure trove
Collared and sleeved in glittering galaxies,
Dusted and sequinned in diamanté,
Stitched invisible in ultramarine blow,
Moulded in magic within a scattered flame-yellow
Breath of pearled magnificence
And spun in splendour of endless seas
Which dazzle the eye,
As the unseen Sibyl of Jewels flies
Without a sound through a vision of obsidian skies,
Bangled in asteroid bracelets and anklets of planets
Ringed, in her fireball gown with comets'
Tail-trains trailing
Deeper than the seas of a million oceaned lands,
Her translucent hands spread and flailing
Nothingness,
Clothed in her star-embroidered black faïence
Draped and whorled,
Gliding weightless
Through the space between worlds....

Over the high winds' race,
Over their glacé embrace,
Smooth space is domed and armoured in
A multi-coloured chariot of light
That dances upon the unseen
Substance of the Sibyl of Jewels
And her star-cloaked,
Star-soaked skin,
Seen in a dream within
A dream,
One ultra-starred and many-faceted night.

Pixikin-led By Star-shine:
(A Faerie-led Ramble)

Pixikin-led by star-shine,
Hid,
Where no man treads
Nor owns nor breathes his dreads,
Nor mouth's gnarl-lipped, ill-charged curses
From coarse and ugly-knotted breasts,
A foulness flung at tree, at blue or carmine
Blooms, at sad exploited, hounded crests
Of time-ground and rounded hills,
At windless, dark-leaf dimple
Of tinkle-rivered dingle,
Aspen-bestrewn dells and jangled flower-bells
Between gleam-leaf wood or glades,
Nor upwards to the metal-cloud, metal-loud,
Speed-machine-paved sky,
Nor down into the cool, green-veined eye
Of mild-brewed, mildew-fielded meadow-mead...

Pixikin-led by star-shine,
Hid,
Where cuckoos sip sly at shy-placed cuckoo-spit
From the spy-green glassy Under of simple
Stem-slung sampled, fluted fine-cut swords,
An ocean moss-bend blend, bronzed brave blades
Bowed to smooth-stone loam home-shield,
Splinter-splay sprays of fountained bowers,
A lush and wholesome yield
Snail-trailed muted moon path
Lattice of sidereal, snail-star powers
That, web-fine, find no use for invocations
Nor hush of wizard-whispered words nor
Bewitched, spell-stilled hazel wines, leaf floor
Brewed by yeast of muttered incantations...

Pixikin-led by star-shine,
Hid,
Where smile-faced, sun-glad violets peek

From their mild-faced stations seek
Mild and dusty, daisy-meek, and scoffs
A cap-doffed, thin-limbed sprite, who
Hums soft a mad song, old and new,
Insect small and cloud-night sad,
Way, way below the threaded needle-loft might
Of woodbine woodwind orchestrated pitch of pines,
Their spiky-towered thrust crow nest crowned sway-tall
And resin sticky, wafting clean air
Sharp and heady exhalation
Pushing up among whited, fleece-sheep clouds
Crowed to azure blue in air-strewn exultation....

Pixikin-led by star-shine,
Hid,
Slight above the mud-clung bed
Of hugeing, fledgling red
Earth, caped in flowing ploughshared furrows
In softed blanket-downs of marshy mellow
Meadows, topped in cowslipping dew-bright moon-rains
Owned by no man curse-tongued of rancid throat,
Chipped and toothed breath fouled in chemical grains
Nor poisoned man-loose brains
Addled of manmade adder's chalk,
And far, far from sunning bark of pining willows
That, with swishing leafin talk,
Yellow-flowered burst in thirst-flown, full-blown blow
To witching, switching touchwood caress
To frond-tip bless
The constant-changing film of silver-birching streams....

Pixikin-led by star-shine,
Hid,
Where an inch-high Summer elfin, leaf-clad
In tailored lawn-cut elegance,
Humming reels and refrains
Faerie-mad, with rose madder grin,
Sits cross-shinned within purpled petal cup,
Sings within the dragon wings of Summer dreams,

And, suddenly mouse-mute,
Fawns a seed-winged glance,
Elfin eyes askew, pinkly askance
At tiny lamb-sprung nimble
Twig-kin fingers' dance,
Long of nail and light of thimble,
Sews swift and deft
(And to the left)
With a cleft and rough rock-whetted thorn
Tailed winding with hare's fur soft and plaited strand
Rubbed and sealed quick
With quicksilver hand and lotion
Of six bees' waxy-fatted sap, an awesome potion,
To lace fine faerie-fabric rent, chevron torn
By an innocent, bruise-black and early-berried thorn....

Pixikin-led by star-shine,
Hid,
Thus this fly-winged creature mends,
Greener lit by clever light
Transparent, of purple clover leaf canopy
Held against the white glare of fire-spined
And gold-boned sun that, slow-foot fast, beams through
Light-head air in headlong flight
Toward a goblin-wanded black of blank lack-light,
The blackest pit of deep sound night....

Pixikin-led by star-shine,
Hid,
Where speck of sprite
With accurate stroke and pin-sharp eye and sight
Splices tunic torn of emerald, a living sloe leaf doublet
Fashioned neat and finished sweet
With faerie fret and flint
While, in chagrined hex of elf-sight,
This pixie-creature, hurt,
Slant eye keens for to whistle up a vengeance,
A sharp-tooth, saw-wind, swirl-wing thistle of a storm....

Pixikin-led by star-shine,
Hid,

115

As complete as is the lightning of elfin-sight,
As hidden as the embered fire of faerie fury
Or the emotion-stifling smoke of a raging, hex-lit heart,
While with a snailsome eye shine,
This whistle-keening sprite
Cleans green-fleshed chest
Rip-thorn wound,
Clips closed its sap-spilled mouth with stag-bug heads
Which bite yet though in the grip
Of head-pincered demise,
Powders all in pollen fine
Plucked from protesting buttercup,
Pads the work in self-heal chewed to a mulchy pap,
Binds bird bone breast
With bindweed moss wrap
And magick's to the crest
Of sky and meadow weald,
As sprigs of sprightly fingers sew and splice,
Insect-like,
Each hare's fur stitch to gather up
A storm-cloud swarm,
While pixikin voice drones a manifesting spell obscure:
"*Come thunderclap, spike*
Hither fork-lit light-point's clash and flash,
Come plant tearing wilder winds!
Hither here maelstrom
With pound of the heaven's beat and drum,
Growth of corms, of bush and tree to dash,
Come hurricane! and hurry, rage my revenge to take,
Cause all yonder fruit to break and burst,
Come this instant! curséd fireball,
Hiss my unslaked wrath,
Come! Strike this, my thorn-bred friend,
Fierce-crash, angersome, its sweet calyx to crack!",
And, all-of-a-sudden peaks a rushing thunder,
Held by dark atmosphere,
Held by cloud track of black
That swirls and spins under

The high blue to overshoot elfin-hiding glade,
Turns upon an unseen, unformed heel
To whisk windy back
And hang stopped within
The surprised, charged air,
Over blackberried cower of humble
Bush, to snake out burning forked-tongue licks
To that plant's last hour
Of sunning, lively life-power of bramble....

Pixikin-led by star-shine,
Hid
No longer, lightning's flame tongue flicks
Again and again and more,
And with an unheard squeal and scream
The bush burns as in an awesome dream,
Its green shoots wither, scorched and blackly charred,
Buds and berries break and branches wriggle
Spiral-tight in the heat, a-fire almost without smoke,
While revenging, wound-sided elf can but giggle
And chuckle-dance until faerie-wrath is quenched,
Laugh to the invisible, impossible stars,
Claps tiny hands in pixied pleasure;
"*Lo!*", the thorn-hurt sprite calls
From its filed teeth clenched,
"*By cloud of Night's coverlet cloak,*
Spike-toothed pierced,
Fierce-flock no more, but by the marbled might
Of my star-bed, midnight black of blackest flower,
My dripping, grave-shroud bloom,
I say Go! Go from this lesson-well-learned
And pitisome briar, go to whence you came,
Sped by the foul and fright-filled, secret name
Of the Unholy Wormed Angel,
The leathern-winged and evil-crowned King!":
So and thus does elfin fling
Out the arcane fear-bleached and hooded word,
And thunderous cloud within that moment melts,
Falls mottled as rain or ermine pelts,

117

Over cinder-stricken bush, extinguishes
All-consuming flame
In a wind-some, handsome shower....

Pixikin-led by star-shine,
Hid,
By word sword, pixie-cursed burnt bower,
As grey-blue smoke caresses fond
The lilting breeze, the gentle-bowing tresses
Of greening, sun-blaze seeking frond
Of gladdening grass and placid flower,
The Summer elf does six somersaults in myriad glees
Beneath each leaf, each shadow-shelter
Of sweeping trees,
And the day sighs butterflies
In wing-breath fluttered flights
Towards the hidden hummingbird stars,
The hunting moon-faced kites
And lack-light, soul black bite of stars
In frozen jaws of slow approaching, sightless space....

Pixikin-led by star-shine,
Hid
In star-shine's unbidden face,
Pixikin-led by star-shine,
Hid
In star-shine's hidden face!

Young Shoots

Wood-limbed fawn sidles up,
Takes tender sip in fragile cup,
Sap of tongue in slender sup,
Greening grain of ovine pup.

Curling frond of beauty rare,
Fern web head in bare cell dare,
Fine branch touch without a care,
Delicate shake of maidenhair!

The Hollow Ghost

When hollow ghost its hallowed owl voice cries,
Drifts alone in shunted stones of Desolation's valleys,
Or wanders lost,
Amazed in shock through the maze of all passed lives
To tip a cobweb cloud in copse or nimbus-float
Within etheric spinneys;
Accumulates occult energies
That hum a hundred hungry hives
Orchestrated fine-pitched
Though there be no ears to hear,
Then this celestial mute-music of the One Sphere
Shall into Universal years be for All Time tossed!

When this vacant spectre's keen
Calls down the blunted clouds
To nest among the cuckooed green
Hills as fallen snow applauds
The rounded Earth in silence, the ghost
It melts away in a lonely shading ache-frost
Like misty coals might, within a colding fire, take
Heat and heart from icicles
To form a filtered dew which ponds
Upon the lowland cuts of gleaning, gleaming sickles,
Blades of an alienated soul in torment,
Then it may slip to you as quiet as quake
Of blood in pulsing vein
Within the flesh pours in unthought, unseen torrent,
A never-ending inner river rain.

And when this empty ghost lies with you,
Mist of head upon your soft night pillow
And touches with you dark
Surface waters with its slight willow
Hands of becalming sleep
So to lightly lilt and dance
With you to keep

Some vague hold on time (and thus
The vibrant life that jumps
A-mercury within the nerve to freshen under slumber)
Then you may realise how this ghost pumps
Darking through our dreams within a timeless chyme
Within its shroud sewn of hours,
A weary spirit that yaws about and yawns,
Breathes a breath unseen through this life of ours,
Is carried with us each and every day Within,
As we swiftly dart or slowly lumber
Down the hidden road, across all clear-
Seen lovely Summer lawns
Of our pleased, brighting acquaintance;
Yes, it's our *own* ghost- and spirit-half
Staves close to living flesh and skin!

The phantom laughs as we so laugh,
Grins as we so grin....

Midnight Trees

Tall shadows, midnight trees move
Skeletal among themselves,
Take air in from the unseen mouths
Within a new moon night.

Frosting sky, cupped receding ever,
Is mauve and deep as hidden
Meditation's thought might
Be nerved sudden,
Unexpected, as by day-fleshed peep
Flash of my sole lamp's light
I slow wend my single way
Home to a solitary, simple sleep.

120

The Mystic Blood

Discover what it is
Moves beneath you; an unseen tide
Slides a rosin bow
Strung in bass tones mellow,
Tunes a subtle flood
To anew inside
A secret earth,
In resonate flow
Through an unknown wood
Which grains below
The stones of bones,
The tempered drum
Of riding, rising skin.

Deepening...
Hear the hum
Sound as though wires in a Winter wind
Were pulled tight-drawn to warm
All flown strings of singing air
And, to a dancing sap,
Wrap as if with shine of hair
In a silent-footed,
Tipping tapping heat of step,
An earthen-rooted,
Mossed and gentle-cradled
Lap.

Discover what it is
Breathes beneath you; the very life-blood
Transmute
As an alchemic lead
Which gilds to lute
And cello
Deep and mellow
Through a sacred vein
In vital charge of Spring
And teeming beat of rain,
Pool of primal heart and welling

121

Roar of fountainhead,
Permeates the living inner grain.
Discover what it is
Abounds beneath you; the simple cell
Holds all power within the blood;
To know it well is to grow anew
With all the ample ways of Good.

Dragon Lines

In perfection of continual line,
As round as Earth viewed full from space,
An obsidian stone carved atom fine,
A roundel anthracite dark, sheer upon the Cosmic Face,
Single circle (of colour raven)
Feathers upon a matrix of jet jade night-flakes;
It soars and floats, blacker than black,
As if Moon's ellipse were a sudden eclipse
Starless upon myopic ebony lakes,
Intense (and subtly graven)
Celestial in sensual contour of the Deepest.

There, cloaked hidden in the open it hides and glides
This Black Pearl golden dragons seek,
Eye-point in shadow cast within a far-flung nest
To twirl across vast vault velvet's deep polished sleek
And plumb its orb soundless to a corner of sky
Lost complete to all and any search of ear or eye,
Matt of skin and mute of mime
In perfection of continual time
While noble dragons weave silver paths to lace
An artless design as they attempt to trace
(With woven thread of relentless pace)
The continuance of perfected line,
Five-starred pathways held in eternal entwine.

The Black Pearl precious, enclosed in open space,
Rarest prize in all Time golden sought,
The Hidden Treasure, thin carapace, miraculous
Though seldom caught....

Nightfire

Within a night-cooled darkness,
Sprawled and sat by our old-log fire
We watched crackle-dry branches
Their soul-grain to stars aspire
As we both took rest before
Moving on...
It was the fullest of moments;
I knew we could not ask for more!

My gaze drank in her flame-fleshed face
All bathed in shimmering heat,
Her handsome hair laced by Beauty's trace
Did the soundless darkness treat
As we close took rest before...   moving...   on...
Within that fullest of moment's grace
We could not wish for more,
Could never wish for more!

Moving On, Later

Moving on,
Later on,
When the skies cracked
To openly water us cold, close
We felt near the fire we'd left behind
And the nearness of our flames
Glowed us warm.

The King Of Flies

A twist in the lead-foot bed,
Twilight of the unused eye,
Slow lope dreams' stilt tread
Under purple sheet in a sweated sky,
Dripping the sound of headstone
Ripping the bound chain illusion,
Twilight of the misused
Crying crowd
Flight snail-paced in city rain profusion,
Sight nail-faced in chiselled bone
As Death waits with whittled cheek
And designer shroud,
Files an appointment we all must keep,
Sure in his ancient harvest-craft,
Calm in his palled patience,
Unmoved, unmovable, as stone-bone
Still as the cold face of a Winter moon
Or as each past moment
That wanes away unhelped
By waxing thought of stop
In sharpened wit and prescience
Of fade demise....
Soon,
And late,
Comes his soft-foot fall
In hiding cloak of night
Or open sun-rayed day, to crop.

He takes his time,
The King of Flies,
To take our time,
To final close our eyes
Under earth-bound hood
And turf-wrapped shawl,
While I, within Time's
Slow-seeming drawl,

A twist in the lead-foot bed,
Twilight of the unused
Eye in solitude,
Await the rude
End,
But do not dread
The flood of that alien sea,
Or our seeds' solid deep
Sleep
Within a vagueing latency....

Bridge Of Ancient Hands

Bridge of ancient hands
Hewn solid silent stands,
Views lead weight ride of waters rolling
Beneath, bubbling on
To flat sand and round blunt boulder teeth
Lodged within its unfurling span running
To the furlong sea and deep-sea sky,
Filament of horizon's mystery.

Where two rivers natural meet
Stands the handing bridge arched ancient,
Shaped of effort and silenced charm
Complete and patient,
Graven stone lain by tireless muscle timeless
Granite sawn by iron, cut and chipped to dress
The steady river's ocean-seeking arm
In mute rock bracelet.

125

A Hat In Wind

The mad wind as crazy as a whistle
Took a hat go sailing without water,
Hid a few clouds for a second or less
(Gulls surprised in swoop-away)
There, in the maddening middle,
On a sharpened point of coast
Out over landlocked sea
Bristled with fish and stones,
Bellied-up to sun and spray,
And soaked its roundnesses with a wave,
Salted and felt the banded brim,
Sanded crown a sunken dome,
Label six-and-seven-eighths
Flapping flag-like in profound wet,
Turned hat over to beach all colour
Bleached with wet salt sun of years,
Never to know another head,
Never again to shield eyes
Nor to plunge the scalp in darkness,
Hair sleeping; now
A nest for fishes, resting
In the bowlered, bouldered bay!

Alicanthor Rising

Alicanthor, the Forgotten King, a knuckle on horseback
Is too bold for rafters, too defiant for brazzards,
Too brazen for metal spheres,
Is looked down upon by gargoyles,
The corners of his sharp kingdom
Carved by crones, honed by their leathern hands
Steel nails a-glint, the softness of a Winter sun....

Thar She Blows!

Spouting dreams in the dark
Folds of bedclothes' ocean,
Waves heave, weave and part
As she surfaces hugely,
Snoring images devoid of art.

Turning in Sleep's under-sheet
Of yesterday's flower park pattern pink,
Dreams of deep bleating sheep
Uncounted, Leviathan pillowed
Slumbers sweet.

Through black facets of jet night
Jars staccato blowhole breath,
Breaks abrupt, eyes closed tight,
And as she dreams of day's death,
Rays of new dawn's first light
Covers covers cleaving
Beneath
Vibrating diaphragm ceiling;
Blank fish eye blinks open
Unseeing
Into twilight's gloom...
She sounds... dives deep
Below
Star-stud, spark-out room.

Then suddenly, as if by magic,
Or by invisible tug
Of strings... *awakes!*
And with Logic's twitching creep,
With a shrug
Of rested shoulders, slips
Off disappearing sleep.

And she smiles this Best of Days,
In the Morning of Youth's haze,
Into her wide life where she is
The Egg of All Her Future.

127

The Collective Urge

Crowd movement of cells
Rushing to growing,
Protoplasm traffic of footpath avenues
Bunches to peak liquid in spore,
In limb, in mushroom cap,
In rooted branch, in skull cap,
In hair follicle, in kneecap,
And they sing, these cells, move in jostled streams
To spread through unthought flight of wings,
To grow continual, unceasing
In their myriad multiform,
To tilt and joust
Shapes of the new similar
Patterns of collective urge,
Questing and cresting
Throughout all sequential times.

Crowd movement of cells
Flowing into mainstream,
Protoplasmic action of gathered branching
Combines to bind in trunk,
In bifurcation, in tumescent tip,
In fluted bough, in swelling top,
In roading vein, in promised stop,
And they buzz and grow in tumbled teams
To solidify a plan of wings,
To soar and sing eternal,
Constantly to change their form and flight,
To lilt and plough
Through free simulacrum,
Designs of living grace,
Testing and besting
Via vistas visioned within
Kalpa's timeless face.

Summer Thoughts

...and it is stifling, the heat
Here, at the height of Summer,
Blest with cool waters of complete
And round glass-globe murmur
Of a moon-water brook...

...and how the waters, in sharp light,
Reflect the clear, cloudless sky
And crest the crystal waters as I look,
With azure blue as of an eye
Which blinks within thin highlights bright...

...and that single bird on high,
How it without effort soars
There, as the height of Summer roars,
Blest with the nimbleness of wings...
O how it makes the heart delight in simple things...!

Watching, Wondering

At the kitchen door
In the tempest,
Watching
With the quickness
Of envy, of fear
Or the barbed arrows
Of painful love,
A simple country girl,
Her face a white-thorn,
Her gaze the day-star,
As she dumbstruck wonders
What earthly business
The cold clouds have
With their sharp, thunderous
Bright fingers
Probing the hills,
Trees and fields
Of that dark smoke night.

A Certain State

Pattern of a fullness left behind
Snakeskin ghost almost tangible in the air
As though hovering where it were shed
Unexpectedly
At an unknown moment defying recognition
Blueprint of a former plan now used
Apparent being that found no place, unused
A frozen and insubstantial thing
That could have been
That found release of a kind maybe
That took upon itself unbidden
To leave
To stay
To stop as its owner stepped ahead
From then
From the unknown
Into the unknown
To now
Without knowing
As though it were a certain loss
As though it were a certain gain.

When those who really love you
Die and come to tell you that
The world has changed forever
Within a stare real and so direct
The feather of your breath shall waver
Pattern of a fullness in whole perceived
The thunder of the worlds
Will make itself known
Announce itself from centre
From the unknown
To the unknown
To now
With knowing
As though it were a certain loss
As though it were a certain gain.

Follow My Finger

Follow
My moving finger...
Can you see that dim outline?
Make out a river
Mellow
Against the black lack-light
Background lustre shine
In seeming seamless night
Void which hides moist most things
Beneath hidden, hiding wings?

See?
There close holds to be
In an obscurity alive,
Vasting multitudes to abide
Within an open ocean sea,
Within its live and clamoured hive,
Unglimpsed; but try! Sidle
A firm and steady look,
Uncover fragments of an image,
Free blurred forms to slither to
Be fleet, seen from the hitherto
Unseen, framed in the polished ebony tint
As if a hint of print
Upon a leaf-pressed page
In the covers of a firm-closed book,
A manuscript now flung full wide
To the darking haze
Of a failing day's
Last sooting light.

Stare
Long and careful now
And well you might
Reveal by your own eye,
To your own eye bright
The fall of a former secret snow,

131

The heady storm and silent-rising grace
Of the elfin-fresh face
Never-ending, or
The sprite of spiral staircase,
Delicate to the touch
Of sighted fingers, or
A golden figure spread lithe to writhe
Upon a coppered mirror couch, or
Watch in thrall some tall
Silhouette ghost dance slow
And sensual amongst your inner stars....

Where Warm Winds Chase Autumn

An early country morning, here,
Where warm winds chase Autumn
Mild across the red-scuffed soil
To tilt and joust the bowing trees,
Their boss of burnished leaves
Turned of polished wood
Or flames of varnished metal,
Clump and clasp their crafted hands
That, grateful in joyous dance,
Weave and sway a prayer
In persistent sweep of toiling air.

Crows swing in sudden to tip and touch
All-in-a-moment the dip of burning branches
Then shower off again as quick as rain
To fly and soar sickle black and silent
Against the blue-white stream of sky
Where, sailing low, those wind-tossed sticks the clouds
Are birds in songs unsung,
Their hammock wings slung brief from west to east,
Horizon-pegged before they rip to slide wide
To roof each hillock, mound and vale
Where the grass-haired fields murmur,
Stipple and swirl skirts of an ocean undulate
Greening sure in ripple waves.

History

When claw climbed high the spined hill,
Dark from the invertebrate
Sea,
Wingless skies cracked out loud and long,
Fierce in bright living testimony:
And now,
Through these, our ages of history,
When we inviolate
Walk to all that will continual be,
When we hold compassion in mind,
Our cells breathe a new life strong,
Firm as the fold rock, lined and old below
Our shod feet, and shrill
Are our chants on the echoing wind,
True words on the echoing wind.

Old Sailors Sing

Flesh half-mast upon brittle bones,
Fish scales wheel around compass hearts,
Storm's rage whips driftwood fishwife crones,
Ancient sailors' veins pump brine
As ocean ups and dives
And their thoughts full-sail full coastal charts,
Their man-gilled whalebone dreams
Sing North Star shellfish,
Salt sea, moon-grilled streams fling seashell starfish
To harbour on well worn decks of salt-capped lives,
And old sailors sing...

Old sailors sing of skull-limpet moons,
Old sailors sing in shipwrecked tunes,
Old sailors sing sea-high breasts,
Old sailors sing in salt bath jests,
Old sailors sing of flying fishy wings,
Old sailors sing as octopuses cling,

Old sailors sing of seaweed thongs,
Old sailors sing sea sirens' songs,
The songs old sailors sing....

Sea wind howls with keelhauled tongues,
Timbers creak liquid phosphor fires,
Tight canvas cracks out loud and long
Songs weed-haired mermaids wail on drift-wave lyres,
While rig-ropes twang tunes the nautilus gongs,
Foam-lipped seas spume up their flesh-white dead
Upon scooped eye-socket
Shores of every mainland dread,
Whilst old sailors sing the songs, the songs
Old sailors sing,
The songs, the songs, the songs old sailors sing....

Moon Over Mombassa

Mystic night without warning floats
Over the sea-sound land
On a silent black-dust wing; it coats
Night air warmth with an airbrush hand.

Only sea and cicadas sound; deep-well
Velvet darkness hides their
Emerald shells, and a belled
Ring could not be clearer.

Moon in an under-arc
Opalescent, pours light proud
Marbling sand with tree shadow,
Boats overhead slow
Across the deepest dark
Speckled star-glow
Sparking sharp vivid illumination
And is lost to eye in sudden cloud.

Old Legends

Covered in cloth the hidden prayer,
Fold upon fold, layer on layer,
Search for words, tale untold,
O speech strip skin, expose the gold,
O voice unwrap a plot rag-rolled,
Centred within strange burlap;
Is it pearl bird or is it a trap
That hides beneath the matted nap?
Use teeth! Bite through the cloth!
Shine light upon old legends of Thoth!

Sewing

I knew that you had patched yourself up when alone,
Had heaped your rags together and tidied edges,
For you had sat and trembled your wishes all awry,
And your inside brought a crooked tension to the room.

Your eyes were frightened animals which ran
As the flight of fireflies, in hithering, zithering zigzags
Over the deserted deserts of your over-powdered face;
You stiff-backed sat on the edge
Of your wooden chair, poised ready to leap
From the ruin of your lemming cliff.

I gently seduced you dance the dawn in,
Took you hardly breathing within my arms
To the waiting doors of a human feeling,
And you, in waltzing step, took in hand
Your final fears, and your warm wood opened;
You moved brave through to drink the sun.

I last saw you laughing light horizons,
Happy in your seamless days... *yippee!*

135

The Defiant Stars

Underneath the seen
Sleeps hidden the heavy light,
Breathes the shielded lean
Lung of our slight days.

Wove of sole intent,
A ghost fabric in glide movement,
Mist beneath a filmy brightness,
Cloud from a covered sun
Behind leaf-strewn tree-branched dresses,
Spreads to half-glimpsed run,
Tips to turn to near reveal
A form in formlessness...
Naked real
Surprise!

Sun in rise
With moon still up,
An eggshell split,
Boat of frail dreams or shattered cup
That once was stone lit afloat
In black alone...
Rare prize!

And the marbled lack-light a blacking pit
Within each solid object
Laughs
At our star's attempt to bathe
All within sunshine golden paths,
But bites the bitter bit
By joining nightfall
In vain seduction of defiant stars!

The Clouds

We meet.
The clouds part,
Smile the day in.

We walk together.
The clouds waft into wisps,
Open bright sky's arms.

We sigh to part.
The clouds clump together,
Weep evening into night.

Mineral You Made Me

Mineral you made me chemical
Thrust of bone and blood and cell
In minimal design,
Mineral you made me animal
Rip of sinewed flesh and yell
Renewed in ancestral mould and line.

Along the rock-lined layer climb
Moved the beast that bred me,
Crawled jointed from the slime
Seas that fed me,
Howled a glimpsed intent
To the crested scarp and battlement
Which led me
To this written moment.

Mineral your metal made me
Drink to think again,
Mineral you made me cerebral,
Bade me drink again,
Mineral you made me chemical,
Made me live again.

137

Dreams

Fleeting images shadow show
Flit across eyes set asleep,
Dusky black smooth mask below
A smoother, persona cover sheet.
Dreams of hatted garden gnomes,
Dreams in boxes painted bright,
Dreams of spatial ideal homes,
Dreams of a Technicolor night.

Shady views blowing fierce
Through deep fold's shuttered mind,
As the sleeper's slumbers pierce
Skies of a special, watery, alien kind!

Dreams of Time's broken bucket,
Dreaming torrid love affairs,
Dreams of 'tall sails from Nantucket',
Dreams of neon-electric hares.

Drifting double in the dark,
Astral body floating light,
Flies out soft as morning lark
In evening's heavy leaden flight.

Dreams of jagged glass umbrellas,
Dreaming Dream's dewed cobweb,
Dreams of drinking sarsaparillas,
Dreams of vast seas' flow and ebb.

Dreams of dapper quilted mackerel,
Dreaming fiery Summer's red,
Dreams of deepest echo well,
Dreams of dreaming, awake, in bed....

138

And I Sing Natural

And I sing natural to the mouthing birds,
Tongue and larynx soft against roof of sky;
A minim doffs its sharp wisdom to early morning
Dip and rise, gait of staggered ocean's space,
Its strident stride and tip-foot slated pace.

Crotchets fin through twig mesh hedge,
Bubble soprano and piano
The milky curds of clouding surf,
Swim mewing up the silent
Bark of trees in leafy tingle,
Trumpet and gong each leaf cell,
Bass notes resonate cleft trunks
Along clef curl of curving coast,
Flange a double echo of a mystery,
Flute the ears of fields
And mice-eating seed grain,
Wish and whisper around sand-dune
And quoits as quiet as a ghost rain,
Or paddle childlike rivers
In ankle-deep faith of Earth's
Brooding surplice,
As I sing natural.

In the bathing air I sing natural,
In night-soothing balm of breeze
Throating lips a-spring
Sounding up through green of grass;
A quaver quavers a warbler note to slip
And slide or smite the white
Wind fingers that tug and plectrum
Wicked at clothes and hair,
The whole manuscripted Universe,
Blowing in brass, orchestrates
The sky-climbing chiming comet,
Trombone's hollow meteoric slide,
The singing strings of moon-glow,
Tympanic tree, fifes the fiddling fields,

Orbiting oboe and shining triangle,
The horns of moon drum and bassoon
The harps of celestial *veena* nebulae,
The laughing lutes and cornets celesta the stars,
All springs and glides to step
To minuet of solar dance,
To boogie fiery and fox-trot constellations,
Ring planet bells and clarinet the cosmos,
As I sing natural.

Drink Not To Oblivion

Drink not to oblivion the setting sun,
Distance outstrips horizon
In a paced and measured run.
Take not days benumbed
To that last shut eye,
For all rounds and rounds again
In perfect, complete symmetry.

If within our life our ghosts should catch us,
Then dance with them at the sharpened edge,
The yawning gape of waiting precipice,
In a Universal Joy unbounded,
And at that ultimate crescendo
Orchestrated to final slip and fall...
Dive deep, full-heart sure into the Ocean
Found brimming beneath fresh-dead heat and heft
Downward in a flight of waking
To will the step, the continued walk
Of your Life's brave-striding feet.

So drink not to oblivion the setting sun,
Distance outstrips horizon
In a measured pace and run.
Take not days benumbed
To that last shut sigh,
For all rounds and rounds again
In complete and perfect symmetry.

Unless We Fast Act

Unless we fast act and turn the tide,
To those who sleep with dark clouds
Pillowed in thunder,
To the rotting sheets of tired and tumbled earth,
To the knotted oracle lain deep-root under,
To these flesh-shored, time-bleached,
Sand-girthed lands, dripping
Comes the hooded, hollow, tree-barking man
Manifest of this demon-worshipping century,
Comes his blood-cake maw of mouthing glands,
Comes his footfall-silenced night with seaweed
Drip of blackened teeth,
Comes his choking cloud, his bitter pith-rinded augury
Of man-death,
Of planet fester,
Of Void bequeath,
Of ultimate tester,
Comes oil-feather *rigor mortis*,
Comes Death's sealed scroll
And our kind's bell will crack out mute beneath
Weeping waves,
Comes the last rude exit and final, fatal toll,
Our future a fossil crying lime in osseous caves
Sunk within without trace or thought,
Deeping beneath our sitting flesh,
Look... pause and perceive it shadowy
Below this last sad-stretched skin of ours,
See how Death would draw an eye-freezing lid
Of corpse bone, running the shift of obscuration, slid
Across all our living stars,
Unless we fast act,
Stand up!
Cease to hide!
Unless we fast move
Now! to turn the tide....

The Young Flesh

I remember my young flesh,
The tawny shoulder,
The downy arm, the fresh
Outlook, clear and simple
Slipped from my easy eyes,
The interested smile,
The unwrinkled dimple,
Unfurrowed testament
Of brow and temple.

I remember the young flesh,
The ivory muscle,
The supple limb,
The time
When all climb
Was easy upward
Into the sun;
I recall the wayward
Thought and hard-fought glance,
One to desired one
At the vivid,
Lurid,
Livid,
Local dance.

I remember the young flesh,
A dark girl with eyes
Wicked, and their flash
Of ebony fires
Of midnight bushes,
Eyes enchanted, enchanting,
Singing with the inheritance
Of an ancient sorceress,
A stare of deep oceans intense,
The girl who gypsied out a slender hand
And captured the missed-beat heart
With the one touch,
The one sure stroke of her

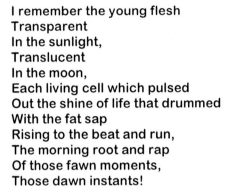

Little finger's slight
Night
Caress....

I remember the young flesh
Transparent
In the sunlight,
Translucent
In the moon,
Each living cell which pulsed
Out the shine of life that drummed
With the fat sap
Rising to the beat and run,
The morning root and rap
Of those fawn moments,
Those dawn instants!

Yes, I remember the young flesh,
As if it were still mine
To own, here, where my old house
Leans into the wind
Or is leaned by it....

Red Is The Thorn

Red is the thorn,
Crimson the rose,
Red on the claw,
Red long on the bone,
Maroon is the grave in monochrome law,
Red fade beneath grey of read headstone;
Star-red the smelt a volcano throws
To scarlet skies of the First Earth Dawn;
But gold are the chains of the Unicorn
And, as vermilion fire from its nostrils flows
Red within its cloud eye the spectrum sews,
Red the blood flood
Which soft within grows,
Red is the thorn,
Crimson the rose.

The Awakening Of Water

When those heads of poets' strength
Met and joyed good in greeting each to each,
Conversed in verse and prose of varied length
Glad to dip the darking realm,
To clasp the clouded helm
Of Dreams' full-sailed reach,
Afloat on honeyed poems a universe in breadth
And cast off far from rock or beach,
Flung together within the bloom of Mind's hyacinth,
To stride gracious over warm nights' lawns to hide
Taking revealing opium
As Shadow Guide
Leading them through Thought's intriguing labyrinth,
Hand in hand with stars formed and fumed by a heady,
Hand-ready laudanum
Quaffed freely,
Then all Water sparked laughing as in a lover's eye
A coronet befitting hobbled Byron
And aerie-wingéd Shelley.

When those heads of poets' strength
Rode in rhyme and beat the winds to wilding wonder,
Plunging fearless into majestic depth
The deeps of unknown mystery to ponder
On that of which All is made,
To conjecture at the soft edges of fine folds of sleep,
To conjure gothic and journey open-hearted yonder
Into darknesses, into jewelled caves' hard cases under
The separating skin, the integral bone, the royal crests
Of inmost thought and closest breast,
Diving deep
To almost fade on
Far oceans of carved obsidian,
Spinning so to leap
By virtue of their own blood in beatitude unbidden
The forbidden knowledge of their special quests

In Meaning, for the thunder in the Eye,
For the lightning in the thigh, to act as uninvited guests
Ploughing deep to gain glimpse
Of that which yet is Hidden,
Then all Water sparked laughing as in a lover's eye
To crown as noble rare hobbled Byron
And aerie-wingéd Shelley.

Autumn Apples

Dimpled rounds of sun-warmed fruit
On hot wood of nutty brown
(The last of the crop this year)
Fallen down,
Gathered...
Placed...
And peach-red....

Mellow globes of dumpy forms
In mottled dust of leafy light
(The last of the glow this day)
Each spaced
From each...
And peach-red....

Silent spheres of dapple skin,
Apples on the straight porch-grain
(The last of our work this month)
Full soft
Smooth
As Summer's rain...
And peach-red.

145

Musing On It

I don't know when anyone died or was born
Not caring a fig for dates and memory challenged
Though I remember everyone in super-detail
The real way they are and the hiding soul within
The young and ageing bodies all aflame
The smiles and tears upon the peach cheeks
Transient flavours of harlequin moments
Set within the mind as kaleidoscope facets
Persistent jewels and woven diamond hard
Amidst the miasmic flow of one-step days
The endless nights in a darking lake flowing
Swift and silent to the enveloping ocean
Waters of an eternal and quieted spirit shared by all
Where the lasting faces lift their primal heads
And open their ageless new eyes
To surprise that they are born.

Highgate Cemetery Revisited

In the boned madness of Highgate Cemetery
Foxes rabbit sleek through hedgehogged brambles,
The cast-down eyes of licheny angels
Are trampled thoughts set in marvelled stone
While whitened wings buff aloft the rustling
Green and yawn-limbed trees' marble long seek
To slender light over the scrambled scatter
Pits of broken slab words split in silent phrase,
Askew amid a former meaning and the mute
Scream of marmoreal gibberish memorial
To the blind gaze of the fallen
Leaves,
And a scurrying ghost leaves in birding hop,
Another in a poured crystal longing,
Another in a scrabbled anxiety of dawns,
Another in a squirreling confusion of hazel
Leaves, leaves...
Leaves wild through the more-than-proper tombs....

Young Leaves

Poetry cannot be made
Without the heart
Without the core
Without the soul
Without the love
Without tears
Without the smile
Without a sense of being
Eternal
And the Muse of Grace,
The Beloved!

Young leaves furl around the stem
Until their lips part,
A smile that is the Sun!

A Waiting

Wise up you man with love ticking timeless
Radiant chasm resplendent and brimming
The breast glowing moving flowing
A longing too rich to curdle
A shining too fulsome to stem
Your tune is not yet timed to the moment
Your source finds no bowl holds its fountain
Your aqueous gold of a transparency molten
Finds no shape for a cup
Changes to harden to silver
Wings which hover within the stilled air
To silent suspense of the muted lip wounded
Your choir draws in its sad breath sweet.
Wise up you man made of love ticking timeless
Your time is not yet not yet not yet....

147

And Soon Shall October Winds

And soon shall October winds
With the artistry of swords
Cut where the white witch spins
Cobwebs over worlds;
And broken bones shall rise up
Their jagged sleeves to mend,
Riddle through cloud skull-cap
Summer's addled brains to spend.

And soon comes October ice
With the majesty of wands,
Freeze where thumb-high pixies splice
Cobwebs over ponds;
And bee-supped cups shall vanish
Their windy fans to end,
Retreat to soil and pumice
Spring-lusting corms to blend.

And soon shall October breeze
With the chemistry of tombs
Bite where the red elf weaves
Cobwebs over wounds;
And silence snow shall gather
Spark star-seed dews to tend,
North gales' brass-cast hammer
Winter's only ice-bone friend!

Gather Me

Gather me gather me
Slip-spin and hammock me
Twist-weave and wing to me
To sail the wild winds with me
Spin-drift and feather me
The wind tide has taken me

The tide wind has shaken me
In awn and float to be
In the above over me
Gather me gather me
Lest all shall cease to be
Gather me gather me
Until the dawn....

Once In Summer 1996

The grass smells of lions
    Something of Africa stirring in England
Feline spoor and sweat of the hunt
    Vapouring up through daisies and buttercups
Big cat odour and the suns of dandelions
    Shimmering amongst vibrant green
Below a pale blue of Summer English sky
    The moist clouds white *pillowing*
Billowing unsuspecting
    Rising lion heat in the distant short grass
The invisible predators unseen in sunlight
    Smell of feline breath and loping walk
A small taste of African dreaming
    Opening an eye under the oaks
Pawing the whiskered grass
Picturing antelope
Flicking a tail
Twitching a flank
Sniffing the breeze
    Something of Africa stirring in England
In a small park by the roaring sea
    A stone's throw from honeysuckle
Once in Summer 1996.

149

Life Continuation

Tied tides wrap our world,
Anchored flesh warms our bones,
Takes its soft and mellow tones
From the human spark
Within its dark
And transient fold,
A flowering, towering
Strength and might
In each and everyone's blackest night.

This kind, kindling, radiant fire
Holding every bright name in choir
Is always young, always old,
Ever it lives, imperishable gold
Flame within fine peach
And transient fold...
Let its powerful light,
Its truly human stone
Flower anew in each
And everyone.

The Growth of Beings

Dawn mists of time rolling, unknowing,
Through layers of tired eyes, unblinking,
Weighed heavy by the madness of our Day,
The whole page of the world they survey.

Steady sight of fossil look,
Through leaves of autumnal book,
To find the dream of Knowing
Through the years of centuries flowing.

Up late, at night, thinking
Of Love; of slumbering, lumbering
Summer's meadows under moon-cloud sky,
Of the growth of beings, Life's Mystery....

Thunderbolt Blue The Evening Sky

Silk in a thunderstorm the weather warm
Summer of the erotic kiss the tumescent nipple
Flushed sunset cheek waterbottle hot
Smooth buttock skin the inner thigh under
Satin slick between the wetted sheets
Gasp of chest rise to breast and shudder
Finger-touch light tremble in lightning flash
Rumble in the throat of twilight round
Curve of hip *(yeah!)* in cradle of body the whole palm
The sure gaze of eyes steady at sundown thunder
Flame orange orgasm in flattened light unwavering
Lit by candles of tearing split electric skies!

May She

She has limbs limned in a certain marble warm
Veined in a cold blue yet hot with pulse
That slender show the living bone beneath true grace
A movement as would bring instant life to alabaster
Her perfect form moves a statue animate.

My sight of her moulds all to an harmony
In richness of rounded gaze the shape of atmospheres
Wherein her returned look speaks of the deeps
Where inner lit with a veiled light the darkness glows
To soft a tenderness as if by touch of skin.

I know her now yet do not tell if she
From fragile sense and experience would truly speak
In like feeling from her smoothed lips firm
Words to shape and set
The coming days in true embrace
So we may in strong determination
Own the continuance of souls.

Within

The sea within
The ocean within
The night within
The woman within
The wood within
The blackness within
The stone within
The sky within
The mouth within
The river within
The forest within
The horse within
The stampede within
The cave within
The stars within
The bird within
The circle within
The light within
The man within
The shadow within
The cloud within
The fish within
The nymph within
The heat within
The panther within
The house within
The face within
The castle within
The sun within
The blood within
The growl within
Grows....

Vanity Of Squares

Not for me cold elemental cement spire
Machine fracture city glass and vertical
Impersonal spear spike sneer to heart fire,
Cold, cold stare to quick of eye inimitable.

Not for me featureless metal greased
To Sunday's becalmed hours and wagered bets
Spit and polish stupidity sublimed on mantelpiece,
Secrets cosseted in hidden mollusc closets.

Not for me the angular brain
Squared thought of the hypotenuse
Equal only to its own fenced sides and vain,
A vanity of squares, cubed and pickled in selfish juice.

Flowing Down A Summer

Flowing down an English Summer
A yield of trees,
Kiting raft of yawning blow,
Murmur in lightened touch a whisper
Taken by breeze to blind clouds' billow
In all-seeing fever
Of the sun....

I wake to arise in a dream,
Light-limbed move through air serene,
Summer meanders
One long gleam,
O how the winds breathe strong and green...
Grass fronds are oceans strange,
A range of rippled tropical seas!

Ginger

Someday you'll remember me in a sunbeam;
I'll sparkle down the dust in sunlight,
Each speck a step afloat,
Warm sun in my heart for you,
Every *'Yes!'* I've ever said for you;
Land light on your freckle skin,
Holding buttercup under your radiant chin
Of porcelain swan down, noble.

Hair of lights runs rainbow through my touch;
I return your smile,
All corners and grinning,
Sweeps of joy brimming, and,
Looking into your flecked eyes
Of wonder, see them singing:
Someday I'll echo in your sunbeam,
Same as I remember you!

Grow In My Breath

Grow in my breath the sleep-shod wind
Mutters a song struck from within
The bellowed cell, chord of a season's yearn,
Chorus of a dreaming eye to earn
Echoes vast branching in a gale
Plucked from the winnowed wing.

Gather and grow in my sleep the breath-shod storm
Stutters a pause pulled from within
The floating gene, hiss of a snaking leap,
Chime of a singled hair to keep
Echoes, vast waves in a tempest
Torn from the trembled scalp!

The Moon Above

And the moon overhead, the half-moon
Flings frost-light cold on dank dark,
Beats wingless
Through birch-bark tremble and soon
Coats an icing glimmer to bark
Soundless...
Hark...!
Moonlight darts and dives owl-feather glide
In the flat folds of fleeting night
Where huddled shadows crouch, or run and hide
Beneath its faint touchless
Touch, its thread-fine, seamless
Fitted suit of close-sewn sight,
And the moon overhead, the half-moon,
As sleepers turn the sky with dream-gestalt
Mooned in cobwebby breath,
It, with diamond-dust hand,
Pours, open-faced, from a brittle dead-sea spoon
Glost sand-salt,
Ghost half-thought
Over a crystal-steeped and silent-sleeping land!

For All The Heads

Our heads will break from out the surf
Of that Great Sea's tumbling waves' clear
Hair long or short and streaming back
Frothing in the spiralling white and part of it
Each expression individual and unique crack
Owning proud prow faces on wave cresting
With tide's power in rush of salt spirit
Along the line of Ocean surfing beach besting
Beneath Sun's fine light in brightness of the soul
And throughout the held heart Night's carol
All the white horse Heads we all hold dear
Moonlit edge to mane Infinite along Eternal shores!

155

Choux Dream Poem

Last night I dreamt a dream which presaged,
Upon jet liquid's blackest black, full-paged,
This verse which now is written, penned
By mind's memory of fleshed words' dripping bend
Across no page spread
Beneath no thought's unsounded deep,
That bottomless, held no sound suspended within sleep,
Spaced as some bardic banquet laid
In letters' rounded roast,
Basted paste cooked in the juice
Of psyche's unspoken ghost,
Or as a flag which unfurls within an unseen wind
Unheard,
Might herald unique unborn wings
As would eggs of no known bird.

After Love

The passage of Time has doors of glass,
Walls of minutes which wile away their hours
Playing games of Chance or whittling sticks
Into cheque books for the idle rich.

My heart is a rag torn by dogs
In their fevered hunger to find blood,
Pulse or beat, to sew their lives onto a line
Anchored somewhere in a future full-bellied.

The passage of Time has windows of wood,
Floors of water in the hall of years;
Under its clocked, curved ceiling of stars
I float unfinned to the gutted horizon!

Something In The Cell

Something in the cell
Holds to gather,
Feels... out... beyond... itself,
Senses
Sea's next wave,
Swell and curve in wet-salt lick,
Fanning foam caress,
Ripple touch on pebble-sanded limb.

Something in the cell
Intuits wisdom,
Feels... out... beyond... ...itself,
Senses
Thoughts in sea-mist breath,
The ocean sweat a galaxy,
Cell star-system rise,
Moisture suspense of warm coast air.

Something in the cell
Shapes a channel,
Feels... out... beyond... ...itself,
Senses
Immeasurable distance
Where veinous rivers branch
Filigree trees to thread on
Behind horizons ringed and ringing imagination.

Something in the cell
Remembers,
Feels... out... beyond... ...itself,
Senses
Space... vast... between... all... ...stars,
Atoms of a greater solid caught
In slow cascade of scale,
Unknown substance bred by something in the cell....!

The Frail Abandoned Muse Of Grace

The frail abandoned Muse of Grace,
Glaze of tear upon her porcelain powder face,
Eyes downcast in mould of Sorrow's mask,
Gazes sad along her hollow rain's softed task
As tumbles opal yield of hurt onto her bone white feet,
A lick which runs in frighted salt
To Earth's full open green lips sweet,
And dampens, with grief's elegance,
Her chemise silk demure and lilt of hand,
That sends wet flight to modest breast
To nipple over mouthing land
In fragrant-scented stipple, flung adrift,
Cast from her vagrant soul
As this Muse despairs, in silent abyss,
Of ever feeling whole,
Yearns within a bone-marrow ache
To assume her rightful place,
A frail abandoned weeping waif
The melancholy Muse of Grace.

Again I Find You

And somewhere again I have found you,
Between the tick of the clock
And the fading hours,
Yes, somewhen again I find you,
You and your heart that smiles flowers.

(And your eyes, blanched in dreams,
Open your blank sleep's seams,
To blunting peep,
In head-turned innocence,
Into the nights of all coming years....)

158

Danse Macabre

Let me speak to you of rock
Beaten by the waves,
Let me talk to you of youth
In beating, living veins.

I sing to you of Life,
Down each winding lane,
Let me dance with you awhile
For we'll not pass here again.

Let me play for you the tune
Of the beating of the heart,
Let us strive we two as one
Beyond Death's final card.

And Time does this to me,
Thin Time does this to me....

Stop; and rest, breathe and smile,
And then resume the walk,
Round each blind bend and corner,
Through fields of growth and stones
Of chalk, sweet earth and bones...
And wonder.

Cleave clear breeze air,
Feel sunlight's stare,
Grow old... Twist... more sparse of tread... *Look!*
The moon bathes in star clouds...
Hold out a hand as full rain falls;
Drops from hidden skies...
Of wonder.

Blaze marble eyes of parchments rare,
To have seen such sights
That bare bright witness to all
In all the world; and clap and sing
To Time's rhythm, stamp and shout
And Trump about
To laugh and love

As the flame goes out...
And wonder.

Time does this to me,
Thin Time does this to me....

That which exists between
Fall and rise of breath
Can at no time be explored, seen,
For there lives Death....

Unrecognised Shadows

Unrecognised the sweet cell you possess
That smiling moves the smooth limn
Which casts a moonlit shadow across eyes
In blink of blinkered view but open
To all in known path the trodden sure
Does tread by the learned experience
The poise and pitch unthought
The smoothed skin a camouflage
The trusted gaze a monument
Until the time the shattered ghost
Runs in open-mouthing gait
The asymmetric path in violence of the sun
The sudden flare and jetted light
The simple thought undone
To nevermore be swathed within
A solid seeming innocence
A nest of thorns begun before
Where now rests the cuckoo clutch
The eggs of hesitation
The pensive lip does wear
Below the quick and darting look
That in an instant stares eternal long
Toward the darkest place now revealed
In ancient clothes its naked form
The deepest layer peeled
To charge in spark a second thought almost

Pure
That meditation upon the one point brings more
In stain of unsure unknowing
The shadow of another limb in measured use
Obscure.

Primal Chord

There is a voice that keens
From out the shoreline breaks
So faint it holds no substance
So thin it moves no breath
An invisibility this voice
Is bare a thrum a ghost
Trace of salt within the air
Just there or almost being
Not a sound along the coast
A voice which tips a silence
From beneath surfaces of seas
Wafts fine a breeze in thread of song
The sparkled soul of singing sands borne long
Through rock and stone the beach-break breeze
Takes this drone of the very heart
This song of sighing souls
This centre of every sound
To the alerted ear in listen
To fall and fall not as mist
A slightest spirit thrum
To tease in lace of play
On and on and long in touch
Upon the stilled enchanted drum
An ephemeral sound in primal chord
A tune of time still and yet to be begun
A transcendence
A suspension
A timelessness in voice
From out the shoreline breaks
In voice in voice
From out the shoreline breaks.

To A Loved One

Be lovely for my heart is sad,
A stillness crests to level and to silent sing,
O how beatific is your placid grace, and how mad
This yearn, this love, this lost feeling
Without you, gentle one.

Be kindly if sometimes I feel life is lost,
It as a deluge rushes and I find no rest,
O how I haunt each instant with your faded ghost,
A remembered fragrance of a tenderness
Without you, gentle one.

Be full of care for the flesh as thin china is,
I brittle through each moment with fear to break,
O how costly seems distance when no one place it pays,
I bow in slow defeat, my tears awake
Without you, gentle one.

Be touch-tender for this love
Has handmade paper wings,
They pearly open pages
At Summer-warmth of memories,
O how they work to lift to you as moon in fullness flings
Wide her parchment arms to try bathe away all miseries
Without you, gentle one.

Be patient now, for in time
All things change their weather,
The clock just marks its own pace when all is final done,
O how swift our wasted years will melt,
As seasons rearrange
Their twisted feathers
To pull us close at last together
Gently, gentle one....

Even Egyptian Evenings Dream

Even Egyptian evenings dream;
In half-light haze under the celestial bowl
The wracked heaven impulse inanimate hangs,
Impervious to lovelorn desert's hard presence; old
Kephera whirrs aloft to imperial stars
As frankincense prayers waft translucent
Through strata of hot stilled nights.

A dreamed top-sail topples, descent of laurel doze
Under the pale riverside trees' spectral stance,
The princely soma-oil air sepulchral dances
In the serene horn of iridescent dreams' nude lustre.
Lyric dart of overhead heat bears beryl opal-breath;
A jackal's bark croaks as sharp as ancient mastic,
Cuts through the evergladed funk mystic
Like a blasphemy,
Like cheapjack chauvinism at an English garden party,
Or a cheap aerosol spray bites a path in bathroom mist.

Harbinger of a drummed shamanic encounter,
Electricity gathers a pall of static in the full-air musk,
Golden inlay of sharkskin dreams' mask oracle
Glistens sand ankh *lapis lazuli*, surface shimmer
Vibrates, smooth-irons a flat water course and steels
Mute beneath the hot canopy of slow-drift cloud,
The living Nile a flowing snake crystal, bejewelled,
The Queen of Rivers, clothed in emerald gowns,
Her maidenhood fusion of flower and fluid
Reflects as a moon the devout coracle of cupped hand.

Even Egyptian evenings dream;
The dreams genuflect.
Distant thunder moves, carved blocks sliding
Over deep-hollow tomb shafts....

163

Under The Moon

The wicked weasel waltzes and the squirrel screams
The howls of owls in other creatures' dreams,
While sheaf of leaf floats on forest streams
The acorn crafts an oak by coded means,
Under the moon.

The girlish griffin grins and the unicorn seems
A tide of teasel on escutcheoned paper reams,
While stalking stork and bitter bittern beams
The beaver rafts a home by concise incisor means,
Under the moon.

The leaf-mould murmurs and the forest steams
First-light dews' ascent to cloudless gleams,
While doves doff and dance
Shade kite combs and keens,
The worm threads a meal by darkly undertaken means,
Under the moon.

Come Metre Me

Come metre me, metre me,
I am the salting sea.
Measure out my girth
Around the coasts of Earth.

I coral-lipped sing my song
While I moon along,
So come and metre me,
I am the exulting sea.

I am the sea,
I am the sea,
I am the waving sea,
Come metre me, come metre me....

164

Opus Of The Earth

The candle-flame points downward
To the centre of the heart,
Heats Time's alembic
From the hidden start,
Transformation's antique
Flow; change's critique...
Blow Time's mystique
To the centre of the heart,
It is this of which I speak,
Where candle-fire points down.

The candle-flame points downward
To the centre of the sky,
Heating, atmospheric,
Movements spiral by,
Transformation's oblique
Path; changes sleek,
Patterns that I seek
In the centre of the heart,
It is this of which I speak
Where candle-fire points down.

The candle-flame points upward
To the centre of the stream,
Healing, hermetic,
Action brewing dreams,
Time's ever cyclic
Dance; vessel's
Geometric stance
In the centre of the heart,
It is this of which I speak,
As sun-fire aeons filter down.

The Garden Roses

Reading among the roses,
Leaf and leaf and leaf translucent in the sun,
Vibrant dancing the scent within
Year, month, minute, moment,
The secret next page poised hidden
Within the thorn, a story unseen
Until the final green line
Flicks its revealing root across to open
Petals; the eye,
Reading among the roses reads
A living imaginary flower.

Two Pennies

Two pennies for your thought,
Two for sweet surprise,
Two pennies for your sweet eyes,
Two for *Mardi Gras* spiced lies,
Two pennies tossed to sun-moon skies.
Two pennies,
Two pennies,
Two pennies for your caught
Birdying glance, two pennies...
Just two pennies,
Two shining copper pennies!

For Certain Sure

She understands for certain sure.
At first I fell word over lure
In love with her down the years,
Then loved her true across the time-locked ages
Which separate her from me in folded tiers
Of earth sweet and silent-printed pages,
While a crumpled time-passed shell, a lair
Of stubborn bones, her bones, moulders
Where I know not but pledge to try and find.
May her stilled headstone still mark where
Her nestled head, her rested shoulders
Cleave no weathered air,
Where her once All-seeing eyes are blind.

For certain sure she understands,
She talks to me at night
And lays with expert hands
Gentle soft as within
A second grave
Of lively living, yes, and a second sight...
Oh, she comes alive all right...
She makes me weep and laugh to grin
To know her like I do, as, from the past,
That primeval stop which catches up at death
And to which we all must join to rave
About in silence; from this very last
All-Life-in-a-moment simple time she slips,
Lives again in my centre-heart and eyes
Without needing prop of bone or shine of hair,
Throating voice or round of hip
As she, tangibly visible, unsilent, skips
To flip her skill from word-beat page
Across all Time and age
And ties me to her.

She understands for certain sure,
She knew and knows the earth,

The nature of all beings and their personal hearth,
Which is a heath, a rock, a tree, a river,
The sheer rise of fluting sky and the giver
Of Life, cruel, compassionate,
Firm in youth yet wisely old,
Which is Life itself when all in Truth is told.
She lived the ugliness and beauty
Of the ugly and the beautied,
And she speaks to me in feeling,
True emotion flesh-fruited,
All of which Is and is to me
All, of which will ever be.

For certain sure she understands
The Invisible, and worked to wed its form
Solid into royal shape and sound of common lands.
She strongly took the mountain road, and,
Being herself all the world in all the world,
Let the World Witch take her;
So it was the world that she took with her to corm
Into the grave, and it was her world of words
She left here within her peopled leaves
To breathe without error;
It is her Life I now hold in reading hands,
That by her art and grace I take
Along with me down all the sands
Of real imagination, in sleep or dreams awake;
It is her Life I hug close
In my blood or in my candled bed,
It is her Life I fold, closed
In a world-dust sleeve more treasured,
Much more treasured, than mere gold.

She understands for certain sure
The fined and refined alchemy of sap,
And sipped and supped well at the clear wellhead tap,
For, as I open her wood and begin to read the allure
In lustre of her lines, my life bites to tail of century

With the teeth of this century's head
And surprises to find another head, instead
Of centurion serpent's tail;
Yes, it is your wonderful head and mind that makes
Me see through a crystal, timeless sea,
In an under-ocean which does not falter,
That I will not fail
To love you still, honest, beautiful writer.

(You call to me from down the years,
From that place where all is stopped;
And did I ever hold you close
In a former life? Did I?
And will you let me take you whome
In a future life? Will you? And in full
Thorn- and apple-blow will we cradle
The Golden Apple then? Will we?
Do you know? You call to me
From down the human years
From that place where all is stopped
Forevermore,
And yet stops not, for certain sure....)

Should Night's Song Fall

Should night's song fall sweet,
Choired of stellar velvet,
Chorused of galaxies in slow-spin drum
To waft in vibrant melt about your lissom feet;
Should milk moon rise tall to fix and never set,
Sired as stars which call as crickets thrum,
Conceived of deep-space web the planet spider's pearl
Cocoon, where dipping sperm
Of orbit-crabbing meteors meet,
Rush her celling nucleus egg of lunar belling dumb,
Plunge to whale-eye core

169

Through her dead-sea cratered skin
And curl her birthing purl
In knit of blossomed matrix across the halcyon deep;
Should all from Earth rise in will-lost carefree slumber,
Where bright illusions show the living grain
Of psyche's deep-well timbre
Grown in young bud furl to lumber rising
At the clearing rain of sun,
Jump in memory sewn as sap embroidered
Or pictured blood does hurl
Through lap of mind's bright vein,
And, as quicksilver fish, leap
Sleek pulsed with feeling's throb
And musing pace of the ancient face,
The primal race and bone
Of brittle-timbered human beings.

Should day not dawn and land to gelatine become,
Mired of molecular mud
And soup out slow to ocean's steep,
Fused of saline marl, of sand-grain snarl and snag,
Of white horse sea-hag wave's salt slick
And licking run, and, fathoms under,
Form seabed walls in city mould of dream;
Should night's throat fall songs sweet
From splattered dome aloft,
Choired of stellar velvet by dust of aeons doft,
Chorused of galaxies in slow-hum spin
Of white dove's gentle wing,
All the vaulted stars can hold no treasure borne above
That weighs as light as precious sight in thrall,
When our raised eyes close-hold in look and gaze,
My love...!

An Invitation To The Dance

Strip the shunted mellow light,
Show the stippled stream and breathe full,
Move a measured, muscled mile ahead
While you smile in treasured sleep
To the relaxed dream of resting cell,
To the imaged imprint within that waxen bell
Left dusty still upon the window sill
Of silence, a soundlessness
Dressed of thoughts in sifting, shifting sands
Modelled of water held in orchestrated hands
Carved lucid by sea-beach waves
To wake the barnacle encrusted clouds
With the rock-shaking thunder sound,
The vivid lightning break of a first thought clear.

O my inner dear, you have gathered rainbows
Collected with dewed trees and time-steeped lakes
To place them living deep within your eyes.

O my inner love, you are built of movement,
Minnows flash fire in upstream day-stream
Light of Midsummer brooks and autumnal leaves,
Flight of winging blow beneath the skin.

O my inner wonder, you the Marvellous are,
You are star-mist stream,
You swim in clear crystal galaxies;
O wake with me to the brightest star
And, poised close at the brink of joy
Within a day of wonder
Made from widesome expanse,
We will dance entwined
Through *all* our Summer meadows....

For The Human Beings

I weep for all that could have been
Stand within a rain of my own summoning....

Oh I have thought how sweet
It would be to begin again
To honey the bitter
Tongue to speak such words
As would heal wounds
Of such agape a smile
Would look a mere scratch upon a graze
Then, on reflection
On gazing deep into the mirror light
See within the darking hours
A measure of minutes thinning
To an assured atom speck of no certain point or act
Where All is in all in fact.

I weep for all that could have been
Stand within the sun of my own being....

I go to where bridges of water shine
As mirrors to the end of sight
From where the old shaman called me
Sleeping behind the eyes
To the circled house where hover feathers
The spirits of eagles' flight across the mind
Behind a forest at the back of the sea
The round skin of Being against the stars
And the breath of the world in stones
To await the rain to fall in the dry air
Above the sacred fire of our heart the one
True voice singing such songs
As would cause the flook of whirlwinds
To be stilled along the full-lipped shores
Where I will see you again
Waiting for me for the first time
The wing on the wind.

For you will play the river
To run across tongues of gold
The clock has not touched
Nor the sun set to bring storms
To speech and words
Soft in their carving arches
In a smile that drops opals from skies
Bathed in the blush of new thoughts
The tanned skin of the hearth
Sacred turn of the fire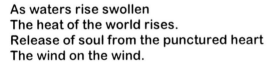
The moon as a palm of water
Reflecting the lake of our leaving
Spume of ocean in the rounded air
Waving and whispering green
The white silence of stars over water
Behind a cloud at the back of the world
I will greet you again
For the first time along the shore
The wind on the wing.

As waters rise swollen
The heat of the world rises.
Release of soul from the punctured heart
The wind on the wind.

I have fashioned wood to hold
The souls of our offspring
At the crossing of waters
At the ring of stones
At the centre of lightning
The thunderbird my heart
Soaring to zenith heights
Rippling through laughing brooks
Behind the tossing of forests at the back of oceans
The brave cheek moving
Above a grin the happiness of Being makes
Ripples upon round sands of beaches
Where rests a feather released
To drift floating to the poles
Our ancestors hold in the palm of one hand

The lake reflects the one shadow
The single image of eagles makes
In the scales of their long sight
Calling to the star spirits along the edge of all worlds
The wing on the wing.

I have tasted tornadoes
In the teeth of tempests the wolf has sired
Below a circling vortex filled with birds
Chasing fishes in that elixir of fluid metal
Element of past promises
Flavour of the fallen wood
Season of sorrel in the eternal grove
Sorrow of a savour found lost
Around the graven mound of scents
The skin of gales once gathered
To grace shells encircling heads
That think of us that we meet
Again on sparkling stars of dunes
For the first time along the beach
As the mind of mountains soars
Without assumption of pose
The gaze of sincerity
Solid from that sharp edge in level rock of sight
Anchored in earth the essence as light as dust
While eagles' breath measures
The girth and movement of all worlds
On a shore of light above us
Wing on the wind.

Speak To Me Not

Speak to me not the bridled sun
Shall not grace the turning sky
where aspens fall and tumble to the earth
In shaken sacrifice complete
Before the blade has cause to blink,
Before the day has a laughing chance,
To paint an eye upon an edge....

Should I Hold Hard Here Under?

Should I hold hard here under the sheeted roof,
Closed eyes hoofed, and tiptoe on dreams' soft edge,
Aloof to daylight as dawn hones horizon's blade bright
To carve future deeds into image
Which day might allege I would bring
To light within its closed fists' night-sealed might?

Should I lonely lie long here under woven warm cover,
A blanket soft as the cow-flanked fields
Where the nude sun swims in wheat
And stands upon its radiant feet
On fresh-lit hills of morning to yawn and beaming burn
Like blazing hayrick, with flamed folds
Of a sleeping form?
And what wonders race ahead today?
Which homesteading turn will farm my dreams
To spread upon my one pillow tonight?
And where shall rest the one-day-older head?

Should I hove to here under the milk-masked face,
While dream-pictures hypnogogic blink to blow beneath
Blank lids, to mingle with the dingled dell
Of day's fine-laced teeth?
Look! Comes clear-glass sphere within
A white book upon an open palm
That floats upon a great sighing lake,
The melted essence of a wish,
Falling water of blown crystal, of polished sheen
Of emerald green, slid with waved faces
Of sunning women who, thankful, slake
Hot thirsts on wistful songs of seeping, sleeping fish,
Or coral powder spread red with life-invoking psalm
Over the salted skin of long-dead sailors' silenced lips!

Should I lie in longing laze here under
The untroubled brow,
Slide siding into the dark cinema of eldritch dream,

175

Float light upon warm stream
Of day-cheating cloud to row
Through a picture spawned by the hidden hand,
The illusion-spinning wrist of dreams' veiled artist
Who weaves sure with mist-shuttled dipping brush
A sleeping muse of velvet, fragile as the final
Ice of a lush Spring's first timid steps,
Ice that melts swift before the brass
Tone of sun-bronzed hands which shake a bellied nest
To release to air the winged and singing eggs of fire
Phoenix and the shining smiles of countless children
Who run open-armed into the gills
Of laughing, flying fish?

Should I stay swathed here under the fur of dreams,
While ermine birds in outside trees
And nested eaves bathe
In a day ribboned in winding waters
Of my dream-delirium, choired in the sounding deeps
Of wells and ocean's aquarium,
Born of the greening dark salt
Of mermaids' night-flying hair,
Birthed of the preening wolf-fish lair of mermen
That scale and twist about in flutes of waves
Between the slates and spires
Of country churches,
Spike fishy the bubbled branches
Of knelling wood and spinney,
Cream my froth-dawn dreams over moonlit
Stains of pointed windows, through the leaded
Gates of sharp-grass meadows,
Hedged in flame-shot glass,
In a misted day-moon morning of breathed miracles?

Should I hold on here under
These cotton-tumbled hills
Or blear-eye bumble and bee into a night-peeled day?
Hey, *look!* a cow's muzzle noses and nuzzles a babe
Awash with light and clothed in clouds of grace!

176

Enquire within upon the child's round smile of face!
Radiant! the sun bursts cheered in prisms from its eyes!
The moon its cheeks, the calm ocean is its hair!
Do I behold the unobscured and natural
Face of Humankind,
Its first real and timely-footed steps yet to take?
Yes, now I see clear with washed sight and mind...
We're children who spoil the Universal playground,
Who bite the milk-filled breast!
My former sight was blind!

So should I heave to here at dream of heaven's peak
To let my dreams wave to me and peek from the inner
Eye, soft whisper to my unseen ear of untold joys
As from a hidden heart
They with love to me speak of wonders,
Or should I rise and try for other shores?

No... should I wake and attempt to rise,
Take my hand and guide me, I implore
Lead me gently back and please,
Please O let me plumb to sleeping deep,
And so, dream-scanning under, let me steep,
Holding hard here under and in peace....

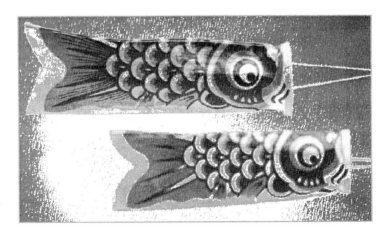

Borderline

Here on the borderline
There is no border,
Here in the doorway
No door,
No desire, all desire,
Here on the borderline

There is no border
Here on the borderline,
No shadow zone,
No light vivid plays, here twilight
Weaves when and where
There is no border.

Catch the shadow,
Sew it to the edge
Of light, to the rim of the sun,
Net a fledgling flight,
Nest it where there is no border
Here on the borderline!

Here
On the borderline
There
Is no border.
I am a window....
I am a door.

Now

Have to go on,
There is no turning back,
You may look around, but all there is
Is gone,
Vanished in a moment in the black
Past.

The past participle heralds its own demise,
And, as I'm sure you know,

The Now
Got up and went!
Gone is the other day, the spent
Second,
The hurried hour whipped by and fast;
There's no real fastening bond,
No let up down the years, the days
Each running instant incessant tears and lays
Ripping through a life, glides
Through thin air or water; all has to go on,
There is no turning back,
Now is All there is, *all* there has ever been, always,
Always.

Testament To Cool

Testament to cool
Winds the heated brow
Flows with such thoughts
As would the world make
Sweet and sour
The laughing tear
Runs wet upon the dry
Skin in symmetry awry
To the pure thought
The sure sight of eye
Beholding the wonder
The miracle of unfurling
Flower the cherished bloom
In graceful turn of head
Where wings full blow
The marvellous image
The natural movement
A beauty revealed
A moment eternal
Your countenance complete
Perfect empathy
Your breath sweet
The colour of bluest skies .

Sea

Gravity pulls to make a skin
Between all gasses,
Those of heavy,
Those of light, separates
Differing masses'
Levy
With a membrane molecular thin,
Transverses undulating,
Divides wet swell of waters
From rushing air's dry flight
And the shining breath of Hermes's daughters
Who, unseen, paint mercury with invisible hands,
Becomes vast convex sphered mirror,
Framed by land's
Rock-hard edge and sanded, surrounded spectre.

It reflects, this salt mirror, night's black lace
Cloud and pearl-starred, highlight moon,
Echoes Dog Star's faceted and changing face,
A jewel-sparkle which presages
Soft lighting of the soon
Morning, blue-bright Slayer of Horned Night;
Its masked white, lazy haze
Cloud cheeks of vapoured ages
Slow cascade, fall into maroon-
Streaked gold and spectrum pages,
Sunsets of a myriad brined, curl-lipped
Sages, in a multitude of lapping
And overlapping days....

Ghost On The Rocks

Jack's shade haunts Big Sur...
His must be
A heavy spirit,
Neat Scotch whisky
One hundred degree Kerouac
Kerosene,
All free
Associations gone and lit,
Ethyl alcohol and grass tea in it,
Creme de Menthe dream-green
Mixed shaken with the icy chocks
Of angry, seething (truly pissed) oceans,
Unpenned break-wave existence
Poems his life's bivouac
Stop.

Now Jack's shade swims in
Through beer-froth shocks,
Rumbling, rolling repetitive trance
Knife-sharp satin dance
In beat tumbleweed waves at Big Sur...
And before final oblivion choruses sink
Sliding, this phantom raises a glass; *chink!*
Toasts, in beatitude, blank verse's holy-roller socks,
Takes a last, lingering neat
Electric beat
Etheric drink...
Ghost on the rocks...!

The Twilight Sky

Purple vines the twilight sky
In seaweed-shape the floating clouds awry
And waving through spumes of vapour that fly
Salt and feather through air's winging eye,
Half-closed or half-open.

The Vortex Bird

The Vortex Bird flies Timeless,
Soundless soars the globe,
Pierces with deep-mirrored eyes
Through dense grey and infested skies
To Humankind's bare-breasted robe.

This Mystic Bird, the Leveller,
Glides on vast unmoving wings,
In tireless search this Traveller
Flings
Whirlpooled storm slipstream....
This flying stone, alchemic,
Is made of every elemental dream
Deep within No Time, polemic,
Times of Change it brings!

The Power Bird, the Fiery,
Rides skull-brow sky-cloud fold,
Heights celestial its eyrie
As from its throat
A thunderbolt
Burns out all in Life that's old.

This Vast Bird, the Water-fount,
Brings gain,
Brings rain,
Sows grain,
Changes and transforms All,
By the Just, correct amount
So New Life's seeds can freely fall
Upon cleared and ready ground.

The Vortex Bird, the Changer,
Is primed for each context,
Changes from the very cortex,
Appears

From mists of the Untimed Mind
To soar skies instantly...
It firmly clears
The tangled growth of jangled
Days of mangled
Mind that holds deeds misspent...
Cuts paths which forward wind
So sad lives no more rent
Thick air with tortured cries,
Torment...
And our Age alters,
Changes,
Rearranges...
Transmuted, old leaden self dies
Into the bright Gold of the New.

The Vortex Bird flies timeless,
Eternal soars the globe,
Pierces with sea-eagle eyes
Through the Deeps
Of all our skies,
Breaths lightning breath
To redress
And dress
Us in our next fine robe,
Soundless...
Silent from the sphere firmament,
Boundless...
This searching, hunting Bird,
A silent ghost,
Host to all spirit,
Its Judgement most
Sublime,
Feels its way soundless,
Reels the never-ending climb
Up the World,
Up the whorled ether
Seemingly soundless

183

To a mortal ear;
Hear...!
The Vortex Bird is near!

The Vortex Bird, the Healer,
The Mystic Bird
That mends unseen
From within the Within,
From fathomed depths of dreams,
Sails sounding plough deep
Into the air of Worlds
From the realm of sleep...
The Vortex Bird, the Whirled,
The Vortex Bird,
The Vortex Bird!
The Vortex Bird is come
Home...

Move quicksilver within all sound...
Soundless....

Magpie Wings

Magpie wings whisper
In oared depth of cornfields,
Black and white rustlers
Within the gold.

Filaments of feathers move
The grain red earth yields
While above azure skies
Hides black space, pearl cold.

Magpie wings oar
In whispered depth of cornfields.

In Deeds Under Suns

In deeds
Under all our suns
Error chases Mistake,
Each Cause to the future runs
In wrong-foot lemming flight,
On fated legs to take
Effect in a scrambled time,
Strange omelettes made
From stranger eggs!

There She Dances

There she dances
My daughter
Full of life and beams
With joy and laughter
Given as if by chance
In those fleeting moments
In the heady glances
Of her mother's eyes
The gliding gleams
Of her mother's sighs.

How is it possible
This Miracle of Life
This enigmatic condition
This Treasure of treasures
Striven and fought for and given
In beatitude of fruition
In benediction the spore of seed
Nursed within the spiral pinnacle
The spiracle of gene the cell unseen
Until the birthing moment
Which seems impossible?
But there she dances
Almost unbelievable
My fine daughter
Full of life indeed....

185

Enduring Horizons

We wrought heady separation
Into a persistent wine
A fermented salt of bitters
Which dressed dim sight
As brightest light of all.

The lemon metal of the sun
Once birthed lightning to cleave
Dark the shade of memory
To blind scuttle and hide within
Split heartwood grain of horizons unseen.

We forged persistent separation
Into a heady wine
A bitter salt of ferment
Which dimmed dressed sight
As lightest brightening of all.

The etched metal of the sun
Once sired sunbirds to leave
Dark the shade of memory
To scuttle within hid heartwood
Grain split of horizons unseen.

We cast steady separation
Into a resistant wine
A salted ferment tinctured
Now quick of undressed sight
As most naked light of all.

They Are Shooting All The Poets!

They are shooting all the poets
Lining us up against the wall
Squinting down their Browning sights
Snarling 'Die, die, Dylan', in fields of flowers
Pungent cordite on the Apollinaire
Aiming to punctuate a finality
Pace a space and bring a full stop
In their haste to reach the end of words
The Frost of our death Burns cold in their eyes
Sassoon we will be Aragon forever
By action of their one crookéd index
Adverse to all meaning of beauty!

They are negating all the poets
Wallpapering us against the wall
Snydering down their Smith and Wheelocks
Snarling inside their hearts' Corso dark
With infernos of Dante and Moore!
O no! See how they Nash their Hughes jaws
Ginsberg! Look how they Stein their iced drinks
Each glass Rimbaudy in crystals of saline breath
As they toast to our Coffin demise in bullets
The explosion of our Shelley death
Their only wit, man
Avoiding all beauty of meaning!

They are erasing all the poets
Splattering our blood to Patten the wall
Poets sit well! Lear back and have Donne with them!
Brooke no Larkin about nor Scott-free stance
Now is not the hour for Carroll's absurd dance
Poets arise! Shake spears and Pound them!
Send them home to their cheap and Baudelaires!
Cast them into our de la Mare to drown
Unwaving at our Breton shorelines
Fling you Poes! Tell them what a Wordsworth!
Poets! Pushkin your *poesies* up their guns
To show them the wonder of our rose etiquette!

Skeleton Fire Time

They will be spinning in the wind, our bones...
Dissolution,
Our flesh made wood within hurricanes...
Desolation,
Gone our hair
Our eyes bent back...
Skeleton fire time.

Blood will be watered in weather incessant...
Dissolution
Teeming vast across unmapped lands...
Desolation,
Gone all built walls
Our minds bent slack...
Skeleton fire time.

Even our remains do not remain...
Dissolution,
Nothing marks our unlogged scatter realms...
Desolation
Deep in gone again
Our Death bent black...
Skeleton fire time.

The Tone Of The Time

The tone of the time
Demands change from the very root
The meeting-point
Of seed and strong line
At the centre the fundamental point
Is the shoot of all Beginnings.

Change the time and change again
From the ion the marker is the plumbing line
For I have seen the Infinite
In the moment
And to sublime seas
Sail upon brave Nature's boat!

Demand change and alter the constant
Within this transitory vessel
Choose route and rudder towards the distance
Work oars and let sailing
Spinnaker take all
From an only island to a Greater Land!

The tone of all times beginning
Demands change...
Hear it chime and climb by the very shoot
Root to nexus point
Change and change again
Within the eternal moment!

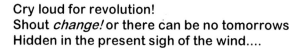

Open Time's vast throat
And *shout!* each change
Cry loud for transformation!
Spread roots into firm found
Immovable matrix anchor
Of new and solid ground!

Cry loud for revolution!
Shout *change!* or there can be no tomorrows
Hidden in the present sigh of the wind....

Our Lady Of Dreams

In the moiré lace of shot-silk,
The mottled bedsheet shadows soft on summer ponds,
In dusty water's sunset-sifted surface,
In blended contours of a sleeping female face,
The light-smudge of clouds blowing fast across
A myopic, lymphatic moon within
A warm night's nurturing, wafting balms,
Hides the sharpest, most cruel edge, paper-cut keen....
Careful,
Lest it slice your throat,
For each and every day all people live
To avoid its parting draw
Over vital pipe and breath, and instincts raw
Run from its cutting tongue and final word,
Close their frightened eyes to its close menace
Lack-heart glint and saline bloody taste.

Night....
And there she basks
Our Lady of Dreams
Sensual sheathed as if within
Knives of petals,
Lilies wrapped by invisible winds
Spiral about her stem, her body built
Of a secret
Water
Congealed in fragrance of summer resins,
Brewed for countless years in the smoking glades,
The rising seasons, of wood.

Mist....
And there she lays, Our Lady of Dreams,
Within the darkest of forests,
Cobweb-swaddled, eye-gleamed,
Cocooned
In lily twist, marooned
At exposed roots of storm-felled timbers,

Rested there upon a nest of needles
In a restless moonlight
Cutting wedged beams through the living
Vertical thrusts of silent trees.

Freeze...
For there she langours
Our Lady of Dreams....
Don't dare snap a twig or move
With rustle or any other sound...
Our Lady of Dreams has razor fingernails,
Silence! or she'll find your vein to change
Pale cape for warm liquid drape
In reddest viscous red and dance in victory,
In glee, to have known you for the shortest time,
Or she'll go to your head like wine, elixir
Laced with poison, free you
From your material prison
Via the shortest of routes....
O she is really not what she seems, our Winter,
Our invisible companion, our Death,
Our Lady of Dreams...

The Swallows

The swallows are leaving,
They are going today,
The chill air is heaving,
Their wings cut the sky.

And in Africa are there liquid pools
Where you will dive and play?
And from Africa do they call to you,
Draw you on your way?

The swallows have left,
They have gone today,
The still air bereft,
There is no more to say...

Stargazey Pie

Poem Details

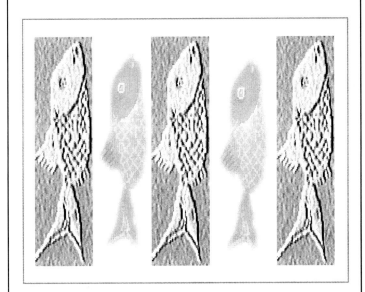

(Plus ADDENDA)

Stargazey Pie : Poem Details: *(200 Poem Titles)*

First. Written: April, 1996, Paignton, Devon.
Stargazey Pie. Written: November 1987, Islington, London.
Opening The Door. Written: April 1998, Paignton, Devon.
We That Have No Home. Written: January 1988, Islington, London.
The Dreamful Stars. Written: June 1990, Highgate, London.
Tread Careful Now.... Written: May 1996, Paignton, Devon.
Sea Timescape. Written: November 1987, Islington, London.
Lava Me Down. Written: January and February 1993, Fuerteventura, Canary Islands.
Portrait of a Winter's Moon. Written: January 1988, Islington, London.
Night Owls. Written: April 1988, London.
Sleeper. Written: December 1990, Rattery, Devon.
The Arm That Holds The Slightest Breath. Written: April 1996, Paignton, Devon.
Crazy Gold. Written: April 1996, Paignton, Devon.
Written. Written: April 1987, Islington, London.
At the End of a Day. Written: 1987, Rattery, Devon.
Reading Below the Surface. Written: December 1987, Islington, London.
Booming of the Day. Written: March 1991, Plymouth, Devon.
Somewhere In Silence. Written: May 1990, London.
Nightheart. Written: June 1992, Plymouth, Devon.
Should I Return. Written: January - March 1990, Rattery, Devon and London.
The Autumn Plough. Written: Sept.1990 - May 1991, Rattery and Plymouth, Devon
Blood Earth. Written: May 1995,Denbury, Devon.
Edge. Written: September 1993, Stokenham, Devon.
With Her At My Dark Side. Written: June 1989, Rattery, Devon.
The Orange Sections of the Sun. Written: December 1995, Paignton, Devon.

194

The Fallow Fields. Written: September 1990, Rattery, Devon.
In Dreams Yet To Come. Written: March 1991, Rattery, Devon.
Sun. Written: April 1991, Plymouth, Devon.
Amber's Song. Written: September 1990 - March 1991 Rattery, & Plymouth.
And I Am Happy In My Sleep. Written: August 1989, Rattery, Devon.
Elusive the Shadow. Written: September 1989, Rattery, Devon.
From a Distance. Written: January 1998, Paignton, Devon.
Related In Light: (The Pointy Stars). Written: July 1989, Rattery, Devon.
An Unknown Time. Written: October 1990, Rattery.
The Sibilant Cell. Written: March 1991, Rattery,
In Painted Silence. Written: March 1991, Rattery, Devon.
In Search Of Temples. Written: November 1990, Rattery, Devon.
Great Age Turns. Written: August 1989, Rattery, Devon.
Time in Wonder. Written: June 1992, Plymouth, Devon.
Star Gothic. Written: November 30th 1995 Paignton, Devon.
Vampire. Written: September 1993, Stokenham, Devon.
The Tumbled Trail. Written: October 1990, Rattery, Devon.
Water From The Living Well. Written: October 1990, Rattery, Devon.
Egg of Stars. Written: February 1991, Rattery, Devon.
Forever Cove: (Your Dream Is Over). Written: June 1988, London.
Street of Dreams. Written: October 1990, Rattery, Devon.
In Memory of Them. Written: December 1990 Rattery, Devon.
Remember Life: (This You Can Do For Me). Written: March 1991, Devon.

Ten Times The Time. Written: January 1993,
Plymouth, Devon.
The Nightside of Truth. Written: September 1993,
Stokenham, Devon.
Speak To Me Not. Written: December 1995, Paignton,
Devon.
Under The Moon. Written: August 1991, Plymouth,
Devon.
Wood At Nightfall. Written: September 1993,
Stokenham, Devon.
Star-fire From The Hat. Written: August 1993,
Stokenham, Devon.
Shower. Written: December 1994, Stokenham, Devon.
The Moon Nests. Written: May 1995, Stokenham,
Devon.
Beneath The Dog-rose. Written: June 1992,
Plymouth, Devon.
All Suns Replete. Written: April 1996, Paignton,
Devon.
You Turn Your Eyes. Written: 8th June 1995,
Denbury, Devon.
Long Shadows. Written: May 1996, Paignton, Devon.
Thumbing Through. Written: April 1990, London.
The Dry Man. Written: December 1994, Stokenham,
Devon.
The Song Of The Shells. Written: December, 1989,
Rattery, Devon.
Sacred The River And A Tree. Written: August 1990,
Devon.
To A Loved One. Written: December 1989,
Devon.
Again I Find You. Written: June 1990, London.
Even Egyptian Evenings Dream. Written: August
1989, Devon.
Quickie. Written: January 1998, Paignton,
Devon.
Should I Hold Hard Here Under? Written: July 1989,
Rattery, Devon.
The Frail Abandoned Muse Of Grace. Written: July
1989, Rattery, Devon.
Unrecognised Shadows. Written: April 1996,
Paignton, Devon.
Two Pennies. Written: April 1991, Plymouth, Devon.

An Invitation To The Dance. Written: November 1990, Devon.
In The Nucleus. Written: October 1988, Rattery, Devon.
Ghost On The Rocks. Written: February 1989, London.
Come Metre Me. Written: May 1991, Plymouth, Devon.
Opus Of The Earth. Written: November 1987, Islington, London.
Under The Orbiting Top. Written: January & February 1993, Fuerteventura and Plymouth, Devon.
Drawing. Written: March 1992, Plymouth, Devon.
Love, The Singing Tree. Written: June 1995, Devon.
Moth To A Flame, Like. Written: May 1995, Stokenham, Devon.
The Desert. Written: May 1990, London.
The City Sea. Written: April 1990, London.
The Thread We Run. Written: May 1990, London.
Out Of The High Night Reaches. Written: December 1989, Rattery, Devon.
Young Shoots. Written: March 1991, Plymouth, Devon.
The Hollow Ghost. Written: January - March 1990, Devon and London.
Thunderbolt Blue The Evening Sky. Written: July 1996, Paignton, Devon.
Primal Chord. Written: March 1997, Paignton, Devon.
Danse Macabre. Written: November 1987, Islington, London.
Joker. Written: November 1992, Plymouth, Devon.
Borderline. Written: May 1991, Plymouth, Devon.
Dusky. Written: January 1988, London.
Testament To Cool. Written: June 1996, Paignton.
Take Not The Word I Breathe. Written: April 1991, Plymouth, Devon.
Nightmare. Written: August 1989, Devon.
Darkness. Written: June 1996, Paignton, Devon.
Now. Written: December 1989, Devon.
For Certain Sure. Written: November 1998, Devon.
Dawn Horus Poem. Written: July 1988, London.
Pixikin-led by Star-shine: (A Faerie-led Ramble). Written: June 1989, Devon.
Only The Tip. Written: August 1989, Devon.

The Devil's Song. Written: April 1996, Paignton, Devon.
Rabbit Tundra. Written: May 1995, Stokenham, Devon.
Dragon Fight. Written: April 1996, Paignton, Devon.
The Mystic Blood. Written: March 1990, London.
I Dance The Dusts. Written: July 1996, Paignton
Some Silent Time Alone. Written: October 1989, Devon.
I Don't Know. Written: April 1996, Paignton.
Her One Name. Written: October 1990, Devon.
The Waves Don't Part. Written: March 1991, Plymouth, Devon.
A Question Of Civilisation. Written: September 1993, Stokenham, Devon.
The Spell Trees. Written: March 1989, Rattery.
Where Warm Winds Chase Autumn. Written: October 1990, Rattery, Devon.
Dragon Lines. Written: March 1990, London.
Midnight Trees. Written: January - March 1990, Devon and London.
Badlands. Written: July 1989, Devon.
After A Dry, Hot Spell. Written: June 1988, London.
December Storm. Written: December 1989, Devon.
A Dancer In Dreams. Written: June 1990, London.
You Should Not Gaze On Me. Written: June 1990, London.
And, And, And, And, And.... Written: June 1997, Paignton, Devon.
The Young Flesh. Written: January 1990, Devon.
Unless We Fast Act. Written: July 1989, Devon.
Should Night's Song Fall. Written: July 1989, Devon.
As Seeds Scout. Written: December 1994, Stokenham, Devon.
Rest Easy Little Soul. Written: December 1989, Devon.
April Devon Sunrise. Written: April 1989, Devon.
Nightfire. Written: June 1990, London.
Moving On, Later. Written: June 1990, London.
The Garden Roses. Written: June 1990, London.

Bridge Of Ancient Hands. Written: April 1991, Plymouth, Devon.
The Spirit-stone. Written: May - June 1988, London and Devon.
I Sing Operatic To The Stars. Written: December 1989, Devon.
Undisputed Islands. Written: June 1991, Plymouth, Devon.
Something In The Cell. Written: April 1992, Plymouth, Devon.
Alicanthor Rising. Written: January - February 1993, Fuerteventura, Canary Islands, and Plymouth, Devon.
A Hat In Wind. Written: June 1992, Plymouth, Devon.
The Moon Above. Written: February 1989, Devon.
The King Of Flies. Written: August 1989, Devon.
And I Sing Natural. Written: August 1989, Devon.
Choux Dream Poem. Written: June 1988, Rattery, Devon.
And Soon Shall October Winds. Written: September 1988, Devon.
Red Is The Thorn. Written: March 1990, London.
A Winter's Summer Spring. Written: February - October 1990, London and Devon.
Gather Me. Written: May 1996, Paignton, Devon.
The Vortex Bird. Written: April 1988, London.
Sea. Written: June - October 1988, London and Devon.
Once In Summer 1996. Written: June 1996, Paignton, Devon.
May She. Written: May 1996, Paignton, Devon.
Thar She Blows! Written: November 1987, London.
The Defiant Stars. Written: February 1992, Plymouth, Devon.
Old Legends. Written: April 1992, Plymouth, Devon.
Sewing. Written: June 1990, London.
Life Continuation. Written: February 1988, London.
Dreams. Written: November 1987, London.
The Collective Urge. Written: April 1991 Plymouth, Devon.
History. Written: December 1989, Devon.
Old Sailors Sing. Written: September 1988, Devon.

The Clouds. Written: February 1990, London.
Mineral You Made Me. Written: November 1990,
Rattery, Devon.
Highgate Cemetery Revisited. Written: April 1995,
Stokenham, Devon.
The Awakening Of Water. Written: September 1990,
Devon.
Young Leaves. Written: June 1996, Paignton, Devon.
Autumn Apples. Written: 1987, Rattery, Devon.
Vanity Of Squares. Written: April 1991, Plymouth,
Devon.
Drink Not To Oblivion. Written: November 1990,
Devon.
Driftwood. Written: August 1989, Devon.
The Moor Wind. Written: October 1988, Devon.
Flowing Down A Summer. Written: August 1991,
Plymouth, Devon.
Moon Over Mombasa. Written: October 1989, Devon.
Follow My Finger. Written: October 1989, Devon.
Summer Thoughts. Written: July 1988, London.
Watching, Wondering. Written: 1987, Rattery.
Sip The Optic. Written: August 1989, Devon.
Within. Written: October 1990, Devon.
A Waiting. Written: June 1996, Paignton, Devon.
After Love. Written: September 1990, Devon.
Ginger. Written: 1987, Rattery, Devon.
The Butterfly. Written: May 1996, Paignton.
Grow In My Breath. Written: January 1993,
Plymouth, Devon.
The Sibyl of Jewels. Written: December 1989,
Rattery, Devon.
For All The Heads. Written: October 1998,
Paignton, Devon.
Musing On It. Written: November 1998, Paignton,
Devon.
A Certain State. Written: December 1998, Paignton,
Devon.
Epitaph. Written: December 1999, Paignton, Devon.
Monkstone Point At 3am (In My Bed). Written:
February 2000. Paignton, Devon.
For The Human Beings. Written: January – December
1999. Paignton, Devon.
Our Lady Of Dreams. Written: September 1990, Devon
The Twilight Sky. Written: 2000, Paignton, Devon.

Magpie Wings. Written: 2001, Paignton, Devon.
In Deeds Under Suns. Written: 2000, Devon.
There She Dances. Written: October 1989, Devon.
Enduring Horizons. Written Paignton, Devon. 2008?
They Are Shooting All The Poets! Paignton. 2010
Skeleton Fire Time. London. 1988.
The Tone Of The Time. London. 1988.
The Swallows. Written: October 1990, Devon.

End-piece: *Galaxy Of Roses*. Written: June 1991,
Plymouth, Devon.

ADDENDA

Printed in other Publications under Author's Copyright:

The Autumn Plough: 'A Special Place' ; 1998, *Poetry Today*,
(Penhaligon Page).
Rest Easy Little Soul: *Poetry Now*, 2002.
Long Shadows: 'Life!' ; 1997, *Poetry Today*.
Unrecognised Shadows: 'Verbertim' ; 1998, *Poetry Today*.
Dragon Fight: 'Strong Words' ; 1997, *Poetry Today*.
Once In Summer 1996: 'House Of Many Rooms' ; 1997.
Should I Return: 'A World For Tomorrow' 1998 *Poetry Today*.
Enduring Horizons: 'Poets 2008 - Southern England',
Forward Press.
They Are Shooting All The Poets!: 'From Coast To Coast' ;
(Regional Collection), *Poetry Now*, 2010.

About the Author

Although beginning to write seriously in 1987, Peter Flux has spent most of his life as a visual artist, working in sculpture and painting of surreal nature. He founded a studio pottery in Saundersfoot, Southwest Wales in the early Sixties and exhibited with John Piper in Tenby, Pembrokeshire. He received an Art education at Shrewsbury and Folkestone schools of Art, going on to receive the Diploma in Art and Design at University of London, Goldsmiths College in the mid 1970's. During the late Sixties he worked for *Apple*, the then *Beatles'* boutique in Baker Street, London, making ceramic sculpture. With Fine Art as a preferred and continued basis, he has worked in the graphic arts too, and has made forays into music also. He is a Lay Member of Nichiren Shoshu Buddhism (Lotus Sect) which has its Head Temple at the foot of Fuji-*san*, the world-renowned and beautiful mountain of Japan.

(The author extends apology for the rather eccentric illustration on p. 192; he says that he just could not resist it!)

Printed by *Prontoprint Ltd.*, Paignton, Devon, UK.

TAKEAWAY PIECE

Galaxy Of Roses

Galaxy of roses
Flung across the sky
Hung webbing aloft
The thorns of timelessness
Netting clouds
In petals of chance.

Cats' cradle boom
And toss of branch,
The breeze masked
In vision of stars,
Tease of dreams' pull
Floating vast oceans unfinned.

Spin me and wax me,
Wrap me in leaves,
Cover me in flowers,
Do as you please,
A galaxy of roses
Prays on its knees.

Every man a planet.
Each woman a star,
Jump, skip or pump
But be as you are!